From the Classroom to the Test

HOW TO **IMPROVE STUDENT ACHIEVEMENT** ON THE **SUMMATIVE ELA ASSESSMENTS**

By Adele T. Macula, EdD

T0308147

Maupin House by

capstone
professional

From the Classroom to the Test: How to Improve Student Achievement on the Summative ELA Assessments
By Adele T. Macula, EdD

Cover Design: Richard Parker
Book Design: Jodi Pedersen

Photo Credits: Public Domain: 156; Shutterstock: Subbotena Svetlana, cover & design elements

Library of Congress Cataloging-in-Publication Data
Cataloging-in-publication information is on file with the Library of Congress.

978-1-4966-0301-2 (pbk.)
978-1-4966-0302-9 (eBook PDF)
978-1-4966-0303-6 (eBook)

Maupin House publishes professional resources for K–12 educators. Contact us for tailored, in-school training or to schedule an author for a workshop or conference. Visit www.maupinhouse.com for free lesson plan downloads.

Maupin House Publishing, Inc. by Capstone Professional
1710 Roe Crest Drive
North Mankato, MN 56003

www.maupinhouse.com
888-262-6135
info@maupinhouse.com

This book includes lists of websites that were operational at the time this book went to press.

Printed in the United States of America in Eau Claire, Wisconsin.
062015   009014

Dedication

My love and thanks to my husband, Joseph, for your endless support, your perpetual cheerleading, and for thirty years of being my one and only partner.

My deepest gratitude to my mother, Irene, for everything you have done for me.

To my fellow educators, who continue to learn deeply and teach well, so that all students may achieve greatness.

To my professional colleagues, who espouse the highest level of instructional leadership and steadfastly champion excellence as the educational standard for all.

Acknowledgments

My sincerest thanks to Karen Soll of Capstone Professional for her direction and guidance from the inception of this book to its completion. Her knowledge and professionalism supported me during the writing period. I am truly grateful for her wisdom and attention throughout the editing process. Her stewardship in publishing this book made my personal dream a professional reality.

Thanks and appreciation to Emily Raij for her editing expertise and meticulous review of the completed manuscript. Her attention to detail is a genuine skill.

With gratitude, thank you to Lynda Zins Dixon for her belief in my ability to author this book. I deeply appreciate her encouragement and friendship.

A special acknowledgment to Student Achievement Partners, which has created exemplary lessons and assessment resources as models of quality instruction. Placing them into the public domain so that they may be shared widely exemplifies the utmost respect for professional learning and collaboration to improve student achievement. Thank you especially to Sandra Alberti, Director of State and District Partnerships and Professional Development, for her invaluable assistance and support.

Table of Contents

Introduction

Today, it is more essential than ever that all students graduate from high school with the knowledge and skills necessary for success in their future lives. As they enter college and travel career paths, they need to be primed and poised to engage in the rigorous demands in their new experiences. Being literate and educated in our global 21st-century humanity comes with new requirements, demands, and expectations for all of our students—from preschool through high school.

According to College Board (2014), "57 percent of SAT takers in the 2013 cohort lacked the academic skills to succeed in college-entry, credit-bearing courses without remediation in at least one subject, and the success rates for such remediation leading to postsecondary completion are far too low" (p. 1). This information is disturbing as it asserts that the readiness skills of students, who have spent 12 years in elementary, middle, and high school classrooms and were awarded a high school diploma, are not at the level needed for success in college and to sustain them as they pursue postsecondary endeavors.

Presented with this blunt reality, urgency exists calling for schools to better meet the academic needs of students. Therefore, the educational program in which students participate at every grade level must be of the highest quality. All students are entitled to a comprehensive school experience that embodies rich, challenging coursework across a range of subjects, focuses on rigorous inquiry and authentic problem-solving, and melds daily work through emerging technologies. Maximizing student potential should be a targeted and measurable goal. Exemplary literacy skills and proficiency require deep engagement that should be the baseline for every student.

An intense focus across the United States has been on the development and implementation of comprehensive national and state-level standards for English language arts/literacy and mathematics. The national standards hold high expectations for students, are academically rigorous, and raise the bar for student learning. There is an expectation of mastery of grade-level skills, coupled with a competent level of performance on the grade-level summative assessments as indicators of college/career readiness. These elements spiral up through the grade levels, each one a key threshold in preparation for the next level of education—through high school achievement onto college/career success, with the ultimate attainment of a profession as the goal.

Similarly, for states that are implementing independent, state-developed standards, their focus targets achievement of a set of clear, consistent, and strong academic standards that provides students with the essential knowledge and skills they need to be ready for careers and college-level coursework. There are several states that have created state-specific standards in English language arts/literacy as well as other subjects.

The implementation of the national and state standards and the initiation of the new summative assessments aligned to national and state standards have caused districts, schools, and educators to fervently redesign curriculum. They are refocusing instruction as they seek to align their resources, instructional goals, learning activities, and professional learning opportunities to the vision and expectations of the national and/or state standards and accompanying assessments.

Assessing the implementation of the national standards through significantly different summative assessments at every grade level has begun during the 2014–2015 school year. Students are now uniformly expected to successfully accomplish complex tasks in English language arts/literacy (ELA) that are vastly atypical of past state assessments. They differ in design and in the mode of administration. The new assessments are centered on measurable indicators of student achievement correlated with college and career readiness. For the first time, across many states, the summative assessments are being administered in an online environment through technology. The assessments are focused on student performance in relation to the mastery of the grade-level indicators aligned to the national standards.

In many states, the summative assessments aligned to national standards are "high-stakes" with the results linked to graduation requirements, teacher accountability, and school funding. Similarly, for the states implementing state-developed standards, they too are in the process of designing and administering assessments as a measurement aligned to the implementation of their standards. In these states, the summative assessments measure grade-level success in elementary and middle school and course-level success in high school. In most cases, the state-specific assessments are also tied to graduation requirements and teacher accountability measures.

From the Classroom to the Test is a comprehensive guidebook to help educators understand the assessments aligned to the national and/or state standards they will encounter. It provides information for designing and implementing instructional strategies and best practices aligned to the assessments that can enhance student performance. Students' performance on the summative assessments will ultimately replicate their learning experiences in today's classrooms. The content and skills teachers present are what students learn. The instructional practices in which students are engaged daily are how they learn. The summative assessments represent an objective measure of how much and how well students have learned. This book concentrates on English language arts/literacy but is written with the premise that literacy extends to every teacher, in every classroom, in every content area.

This book is a testament to implementing a curriculum that is standards based in accordance with high-quality classroom instruction focused on the highest level of student learning. Student learning objectives must be aligned with the standards and clearly define what students should know and be able to do. Instructional activities must correspondingly be designed to actively engage students in developing conceptual understandings, increase procedural skills and knowledge, and apply learning to new situations. Formative assessment to inform future planning and instruction is foundational to this work.

From the Classroom to the Test is a teacher-focused book. We are all teachers, and this is written for the practitioner. Since the summative ELA assessments are not designed in a formulaic way that encourages rote practices and the assessments do not stand apart from the work of teachers in their classrooms, this book focuses on information, strategies, tips, and techniques centered in best practices in literacy that can be employed in classrooms and incorporated into daily lessons.

Educational experiences at the school and classroom levels must foster authentic learning, engage students intently in the work of the grade level, and provide interventions and enrichment opportunities so that all students will be supported beyond their own expectations to higher levels of knowledge.

The summative ELA assessments clearly articulate that students must be proficient readers and writers. Additionally, they are charged with being effective communicators, complex problem-solvers, and producers of quality work. Most importantly, students need to be critical thinkers who can work with independence and confidence. The suggestions throughout the book match these goals.

Each of the chapters in *From the Classroom to the Test* discusses a component of the assessment and provides background information, effective instructional practices, and classroom strategies. The apple icon indicates 10 classroom strategies.

Chapter 1 focuses on the importance of reading comprehension and text complexity. It concentrates on the importance of robust readers of both literature and high-quality informational texts. It provides classroom strategies for teachers to use to build stamina, skills, and self-sufficiency with complex text.

Chapter 2 explores the concepts of close reading, using evidence from a text, and text-dependent questions as methods to deepen students' comprehension of complex text. These approaches are of primary importance as the reading passages on the assessments require focused engagement with the author's purpose and meaning. Moreover, most questions on the assessments require students to support their responses with direct evidence from the text.

Chapter 3 delves into the importance of developing and expanding vocabulary because a student's ability to read and understand words that progressively increase in complexity is a factor vital to school growth. Words used in the educational setting are different from words commonly used in everyday situations. For students to think academically and be poised for school success, they must be familiar with the words that are considered to be part of these specialized vocabularies. Grade-level academic words and content-specific words that students encounter in written texts—both literature and informational—will represent the range of vocabulary with which students will interact on the assessments.

Chapter 4 concentrates on quality writing. Multiple writing tasks will comprise the performance-assessment component of the tests and will require the construction of several essays. The essays will be based on evidence extracted from relevant text sources, including multimedia sources. There are three broad rhetorical writing purposes: opinion/argument, informational/explanatory, and narrative.

Chapter 5 looks at how the summative ELA assessments will incorporate media representations of literary works as well as visual and graphical representations of informational text. They will be paired with traditional text passages, and students will be expected to comprehend each text and answer several text-dependent questions about each piece.

Chapter 6 discusses how conversation, productive talk, and critical listening serve as foundational elements of communication and lead to building skills in reading and writing. This chapter provides examples of speaking and listening activities in the classroom to bridge the connection to improved reading and writing.

Collectively these chapters bring together the elements on which the summative ELA assessments will concentrate. *From the Classroom to the Test* is meant to view the assessments from the broadest terms in order to focus closely on those classroom practices that will make a difference.

Included in the last section of the book are samples of texts and examples of questions similar to items found on the summative ELA assessments. These are offered so that teachers can more efficiently prepare students to effectively demonstrate the skills and understandings critical for success on these assessments, but most importantly, in future college, career, and life settings. These samples support the goals of state-level assessments as well.

The concept of this book is to provide practitioners with helpful and reliable information that can guide them forward by deepening their knowledge about literacy practices and how the summative ELA assessments are designed.

Educators committed to the academic success of their students are presently engaged in much of what is required. With certainty, their professionalism and best practices will spur them to continue to work deeply toward these new goals. I hope this book serves educators well. As this book is in development, hundreds of thousands of students are taking the summative assessments for the first time. I am looking forward to students' success on the assessments and teachers' success through their continued hard work, ongoing professional learning, and enhanced collaboration with colleagues to ensure that our students receive the education they deserve.

CHAPTER 1:
Increasing Reading Comprehension: Text Complexity in Literary and Informational Texts

"Readers become better readers by reading" is a familiar statement often repeated by teachers, parents, and experts. I would like to amend this thought so that it would state "Readers become better readers by reading *and* understanding what they read." Reading is more than sounding out letters or reciting words in sequence as they appear on a page. It is critically important for readers of all ages, at all grade levels, to understand the meaning of the words, know the vocabulary, be familiar with the genre, grasp the nuances of the style, and figure out the meaning of the words that have been constructed as text. Reading is *comprehending* what the author has written.

Comprehension involves understanding the meaning of words in context, while connecting the words with their implication in sentences; linking related thoughts from the sentences into paragraphs; and uniting the ideas, topics, or subject matter into pages, chapters, and books. Reading books *with* comprehension builds the richness of a student's world far beyond the limitations of their physical location by expanding boundaries into vast and new experiences that are infinite. Reading without understanding is an act that is not worth a student's time or effort. Reading with understanding makes all the difference in student success, student learning, and a student's love of reading.

This chapter begins with a focus on the importance of increasing students' reading comprehension by building strong content knowledge across a broad range of subjects. In today's classrooms, students are expected to engage with substantive works appropriate for their grade level that are high quality, varied, and related to the subject areas of study. A student's ability to read and understand texts that progressively increase in complexity as he or she advances through school is a factor vital to school growth.

The chapter centers on text complexity, the importance of robust reading of works of literature and high-quality informational texts, and garnering a deep understanding of the text through reasoning and the use of evidence. Also included are effective classroom strategies for teachers to use as part of their inventory of instructional methods to build stamina, skills, and self-sufficiency with complex text.

Summative Assessments: What to Expect

Focus on Text Complexity

Summative ELA assessments will require that students independently read complex texts—both literary and informational. The passages will represent grade-level-and-above reading proficiency. Therefore, proficient performance on the assessments presumes that students will be able to comprehend the information presented in the passages. These passages usually represent knowledge from content areas at the students' grade level. Content in science, social studies (history, geography, and civics), health, and the arts will comprise the passages. Having read the passage, students will then be expected to analyze and synthesize information from the text to answer several multipart questions that indicate their understanding.

Beginning at the earliest grades in which the summative ELA assessments are given—usually grade three—it is expected that students will be given more than one text passage (two or three) to read and comprehend. The tasks will require students to analyze information from each passage, answer several questions about each passage, and then synthesize information from several passages to complete an assessment task.

There are new question types being introduced on the summative ELA assessments. One question type involves two-part questions in which students must provide the correct answer via a "selected-response" format in the first question, followed by a second question in which students identify one or more evidence statements from the text as reasoning for their selected answers. This question type is commonly referred to as "evidence-based selected response."

Another question type that students will see on the assessments focuses on selecting a correct response, providing evidence, and then responding to the question in a format that is technology driven. These questions involve manipulating text on the screen and highlighting, dragging and dropping, or sequencing responses in a fashion that is prominently visual. This question type is typically called "technology-enhanced selected response."

Students will also be posed with *prose-constructed response* questions and tasks. These tasks will be performance based and require students to provide an extended written response that answers the question, task, etc. after having read several paired text passages, including multimedia format selections. These responses will be grounded in authentic research and reflect students' analysis, evaluation, and synthesis of information they read as a complete final written product. The prose-constructed response products may include narrative writing, informational/explanatory writing, and/or opinion/argument writing.

Future chapters in the book will focus on specific aspects of the summative ELA assessments. I wish to provide you with an upfront look at what to think about as you read the remainder of this chapter to help you consider the instruction focused on the goals of the summative ELA assessments and, subsequently, career and college readiness.

Why Is Reading Comprehension Important?

Today's students are poised to attend college in greater numbers than in past decades. More opportunities for students to become entrepreneurs are available based on technology-forward globalization. Workforce employment and professional responsibilities demand that workers embrace a learning-oriented perspective. Preparing all students for success in college and the 21st-century workplace is the cumulative goal of the effort and work at the elementary, middle, and high school levels.

This goal requires dynamic students who are highly motivated to do well in school. Reading success is integral to developing students expected to engage enthusiastically in their learning, energetically focus on high academic success, and actively study and complete work, projects, and assignments. In order for students to perform effectively in college and career situations, they must engage with and comprehend increasingly complex texts as they progress through the grades, mastering skills as they proceed incrementally through their grade-level and school-wide experiences.

When students move up to the next grade level—and most significantly, when they graduate from high school—they must be able to read independently and proficiently, comprehend a variety of texts of increasing complexity easily and comfortably, and extend and apply what they have learned to new situations, projects, problems, and experiences. This is so they can navigate the level and complexity of texts universally encountered throughout college courses, technical education, career paths, and adult life experiences.

Reading comprehension embodies many skills. Each of the skills has importance as a stand-alone skill; however, when the skills coalesce seamlessly and are clearly evidenced in students' conceptual understanding and demonstration of knowledge, then learning has occurred. Students who can apply this knowledge with predictability in new and novel situations become stronger and more fluent readers, widen their experiences, and expand their views of the world.

This chart identifies comprehension skills that can be taught and applied to all reading situations. These skills include:

Before Reading	During Reading	After Reading
Articulates purpose/reason for reading the text Previews the text (scans chapter and section headings; examines illustrations, tables, and figures) to build a mental picture, image, or map of the content Identifies the topic Sets specific goals, expectations or outcomes by reading the selection	Uses prior knowledge of the topic to connect with the text and more fully understand the meaning of the text Makes and adjusts predictions using the text to validate Makes inferences and supports with evidence Checks for understanding Uses text features (titles, headings, captions, etc.) Distinguishes between fact and opinion Finds the main idea, important facts, and supporting details Uses strategies to define the meaning of unknown words Rereads and asks questions throughout the reading Determines and analyzes the author's purpose Draws conclusions Understands bias Delves back and forth in the text to check facts, answer questions, etc.	Looks back to the text and rereads sections to clarify understanding, clear up confusion, or more fully understand content Retells the story in own words Summarizes key ideas of the text, including identifying the main idea; discusses how the ideas are coherently united Continues to think about the text and the relation of its ideas or content to previous reading or own knowledge and experience Looks for cause-and-effect relationships

Teachers in grades three through eight are truly all teachers of reading. Regardless of the content area for which a teacher is responsible, every teacher must employ a repertoire of reading skills and strategies, enabling students to grow exponentially in reading ability and proficiency. The manifestation of reading proficiency is exhibited both in and beyond the ELA classroom. The demonstration of students' articulation with content-focused reading materials in the social studies, science, health, technical subjects, and arts classrooms illustrates coherence with consistency across subject areas and replicates real-world connections to learning.

Each grade-level teacher needs to utilize complex text as a method of stretching students to achieve greater success in tackling difficult vocabulary words, complicated sentences, and challenging texts. Students need to rely on a collection of strategies that they can apply as they learn to become better readers—readers who make sense of challenging, dense texts at their grade level and above.

According to Pressley (2000), "The case is very strong that teaching elementary, middle school, and high school students to use a repertoire of comprehension strategies increases their comprehension of text. Teachers should model and explain comprehension strategies, have their students practice using such strategies with teacher support, and let students know they are expected to continue using the strategies when reading on their own. Such teaching should occur across every school day, for as long as required to get all readers using the strategies independently—which means including it in reading instruction for years."

Types of Informational Texts

Informational text straightforwardly provides facts and delivers information. The focus is on dispensing knowledge that educates the reader. Informational text is generated in many different formats. These include books, textbooks, magazines, handouts, brochures, journal articles, technical texts (directions, forms, and information displayed in graphs, charts, or maps), and Internet resources. Informational text covers many different topics and is located in resources related to history, social studies, science, the arts, and technical subjects.

Expository text is a type of informational text. Boutelier (2015) states that expository writing has "the purpose of exposing the truth through a reliable source. True and deliberate expository text will focus on educating its reader. Other descriptors of exposition are clear, concise, and organized writing. Expository text gets to the point quickly and efficiently." It is based in the author's research of a topic and written for the purpose of informing the reader. It is fact based and focused. Expository texts can include informational guides, recipes, self-help books, and instruction lists.

Literary nonfiction is classified as a type of informational text. Literary nonfiction includes autobiographies, biographies, memoirs, personal essays, speeches, opinion pieces, essays about art or literature, journalism, and historical, scientific, technical, or economic accounts (including digital sources) written for a broad audience.

Why Does Text Complexity Matter?

The complexity of what students can read is the greatest predictor of success in college, according to American College Testing (ACT, 2006). College students are expected to independently read complex texts, particularly informational texts that are connected to content-based, technical courses. In the report, *Reading Between the Lines*, "what distinguished the performance of students who had earned the benchmark score or better on the ACT from those who had not was not their relative ability to making inferences while reading or answering questions. The clearest differentiator was students' ability to answer questions associated with complex texts" (p. 16).

To elaborate a bit more on this issue, Liben (2010) in *Why Complex Text Matters* states, "The texts students are provided in school to read K–12 are not of sufficient complexity to prepare them for college or career readiness. In addition, expository text, the overwhelmingly dominant form of career and college reading, constitutes a minute portion of what students are asked to read in precollegiate education. When it is read, it is over scaffolded by teachers, and taught superficially (read these pages, and find the answers). Far too many students are not only ill prepared cognitively for the demands this type of text presents, but are unaware there is even a problem, aside from how boring their informational texts seem to be. ...they were blind-sided by tasks they could not perform on text passages they had never been equipped to encounter" (p. 3).

This means that students in elementary and middle grades need to engage more often and more purposefully with informational text. Informational text is harder for students to comprehend than narrative text, and students need more practice interacting with the genre. According to Shanahan (2013), "..informational text is usually organized differently from literary text. Informational text is more likely to use problem-solution, cause-effect, and compare-contrast rhetorical structures....Text features differ, too. (When was the last time you saw bullet points in a poem?) Bold print, italics, headings and subheadings, and sidebars are all more common in informational text. Text guides such as tables of contents and indexes, for example, differ in important ways, as do illustrations and graphics and the roles they play" (p. 14). Additionally, informational text may incorporate dense information, be about an unfamiliar or difficult topic, and feature uncommon vocabulary.

In today's classrooms, interacting with informational text is critical to success in later educational experiences. Nonfiction, in the form of informational and expository texts, makes up the vast majority of required reading in college and the workplace. As students move through the grades, they encounter more difficult textbooks and increased numbers and types of informational text, particularly in content-area courses, such as social studies, science, health, mathematics, and the arts. High-quality informational texts that are content rich, exhibit exceptional craft and thought, and provide useful information should be chosen to align with grade-level curriculum and instructional goals. This strategy supports students learning how to read different types of informational text.

The authors of the Common Core State Standards (2010) tell us, "Current trends suggest that if students cannot read challenging texts with understanding—if they have not developed the skill, concentration, and stamina to read such texts—they will read less, in general. In particular, if students cannot read complex expository text to gain information, they will likely turn to text-free or text-light sources, such as video, podcasts, and tweets. These sources, while not without value, cannot capture the nuance, subtlety, depth, or breadth of ideas developed through complex text" (National Governors Association Center for Best Practices and Council of Chief State School Officers, p. 4).

As a result, an encompassing goal is for all students at all grade levels to gain both general knowledge and discipline-specific expertise. Students are expected to increase their reading comprehension skills by using grade-appropriate literary and informational texts across the range of content areas—science (earth, physical, and life sciences), history/social studies, civics, economics, geography, mathematics, comprehensive health, the arts (e.g., music and art history), and career/technical education career pathways (e.g., carpentry, engineering, and hospitality). Each of these content areas is plentiful with important content; innovative, thought-provoking concepts; and a wealth of new knowledge for students. The interaction with grade-level texts anticipates greater student interest, engagement, communication, and deep involvement with the specific content.

Text Complexity and National Standards

The Common Core State Standards have tackled the "what" and "how" students read by interweaving these aspects and providing clear guidance on classroom practice.

The content areas have risen to a renewed level of significance now that the Common Core State Standards (CCSS) champion the use of informational texts, placing great emphasis on students building knowledge from that reading. It is a clear expectation that students would be engaged in important reading across all of the subjects in which they are enrolled in a given year. This broadens the emphasis on reading in all of the content-area subjects.

As students move up the grades, there is an increasing shift toward reading more nonfiction and informational text. The engagement balance levels of literature and informational text is 50 percent / 50 percent in kindergarten through fifth grade. However, as students move into middle and high school, there is much greater attention placed on informational text, including literary nonfiction. In grades six through 12, the shift expects a reallocation to 70 percent informational text and 30 percent literature—far different from what has been traditionally accepted practice (Student Achievement Partners, slide 17, 2015).

In all courses at the middle and high school levels, this redistribution or shift to informational text is triggering dramatic changes in curriculum expectations, selection of textbooks and resources, development of reading lists, and the types of extended texts being read as part of a grade level or course's required reading. In upper grades (six through 12), a premium is now placed on students interacting with informational text in all of their classes—not just the ELA classroom.

The CCSS define text complexity as three equally important interconnected elements. The elements comprise a "model for determining how easy or difficult a particular text is to read" (Appendix A, p. 4). The elements of the model are:

1. *Qualitative dimensions of text complexity:* In the standards, *qualitative dimensions* and *qualitative factors* refer to those aspects of text complexity best measured or only measurable by an attentive human reader, such as levels of meaning or purpose, structure, language conventionality and clarity, and knowledge demands.

2. *Quantitative dimensions of text complexity:* The terms *quantitative dimensions* and *quantitative factors* refer to those aspects of text complexity, such as word length or frequency, sentence length, and text cohesion, that are difficult—if not impossible—for a human reader to evaluate efficiently, especially in long texts, and are thus today typically measured by computer software.

3. *Reader and task considerations:* While the prior two elements of the model focus on the inherent complexity of text, variables specific to particular readers (such as motivation, knowledge, and experiences) and to particular tasks (such as purpose and the complexity of the task assigned and the questions posed) must also be considered when determining whether a text is appropriate for a given student. Such assessments are best made by teachers employing their professional judgment, experience, and knowledge of their students and the subject.

In the CCSS, Reading Standard 10 provides a vertical progression of complexity that spirals up through the grades. Student skill development related to reading and comprehending informational texts proficiently and independently is structured as grade-by-grade requisites for increasing text complexity.

Equal emphasis is placed on the quality and sophistication of what students read as well as students' reading proficiency and skill. The expectation is for students in all grades to engage with a variety of informational texts across content areas, beginning in kindergarten and concluding in grade 12. In keeping with this book's purpose, the following charts highlight the specifications for grade levels three through eight.

Reading: Informational Text — Range of Reading and Level of Text Complexity	
Source: Common Core State Standards (2010)	
CCR Anchor Standard 10: Read and comprehend complex literary and informational texts independently and proficiently.	
Grade	**Grade-Specific Standard**
Grade 3	By the end of the year, read and comprehend informational texts, including history/social studies, science, and technical texts, at the high end of the grades 2–3 text complexity band independently and proficiently. (CCSS.ELA-Literacy.RI.3.10)
Grade 4	By the end of year, read and comprehend informational texts, including history/social studies, science, and technical texts, in the grades 4–5 text complexity band proficiently, with scaffolding as needed at the high end of the range. (CCSS.ELA-Literacy.RI.4.10)
Grade 5	By the end of the year, read and comprehend informational texts, including history/social studies, science, and technical texts, at the high end of the grades 4–5 text complexity band independently and proficiently. (CCSS.ELA-Literacy.RI.5.10)
Grade 6	By the end of the year, read and comprehend literary nonfiction in the grades 6–8 text complexity band proficiently, with scaffolding as needed at the high end of the range. (CCSS.ELA-Literacy.RI.6.10)
Grade 7	By the end of the year, read and comprehend literary nonfiction in the grades 6–8 text complexity band proficiently, with scaffolding as needed at the high end of the range. (CCSS.ELA-Literacy.RI.7.10)
Grade 8	By the end of the year, read and comprehend literary nonfiction at the high end of the grades 6–8 text complexity band independently and proficiently. (CCSS.ELA-Literacy.RI.8.10)

The infusion of informational text will have implications for all teachers providing instruction in various content areas by bringing cohesion to the breadth of what students read *across all of their classes* and significantly increasing students' reading of informational texts—both short and long passages, etc. However, teachers must also continue to rely on literature for deepening reading comprehension. Literature has been the foundational bedrock of English language arts/literacy programs. If we lose this vital connection to worthy and notable literary works studied at various grade levels, students will lose the opportunity to study and enjoy the beauty of the offerings.

It is essential that high-quality literature continue to be a central focus of an English language arts/literacy program or course. According to Hiebert (2012), "Literature deals with the human condition...the purpose of literature is to convey themes about the human experience—themes of survival, courage, family ties, and the joys and perils of growing up. Some text may not have the most profound themes—especially the texts of beginning reading but true literature, even in picture books, grapples with the great themes of human experience, as the individual's relationship to family, community, and even morality."

Accordingly, CCSS Reading Standard 10 encompasses literature. The vertical progression through the grades similarly relates to reading and comprehending literary texts proficiently and independently.

Reading: Literature — Range of Reading and Level of Text Complexity	
Source: Common Core State Standards (2010)	
CCR Anchor Standard 10: Read and comprehend complex literary and informational texts independently and proficiently.	
Grade	**Grade-Specific Standard**
Grade 3	By the end of the year, read and comprehend literature, including stories, dramas, and poetry, at the high end of the grades 2–3 text complexity band independently and proficiently. (CCSS.ELA-Literacy.RL.3.10)
Grade 4	By the end of the year, read and comprehend literature, including stories, dramas, and poetry, in the grades 4–5 text complexity band proficiently, with scaffolding as needed at the high end of the range. (CCSS.ELA-Literacy.RL.4.10)
Grade 5	By the end of the year, read and comprehend literature, including stories, dramas, and poetry, at the high end of the grades 4–5 text complexity band independently and proficiently. (CCSS.ELA-Literacy.RL.5.10)
Grade 6	By the end of the year, read and comprehend literature, including stories, dramas, and poems, in the grades 6–8 text complexity band proficiently, with scaffolding as needed at the high end of the range. (CCSS.ELA-Literacy.RL.6.10)
Grade 7	By the end of the year, read and comprehend literature, including stories, dramas, and poems, in the grades 6–8 text complexity band proficiently, with scaffolding as needed at the high end of the range. (CCSS.ELA-Literacy.RL.7.10)
Grade 8	By the end of the year, read and comprehend literature, including stories, dramas, and poems, at the high end of grades 6–8 text complexity band independently and proficiently. (CCSS.ELA-Literacy.RL.8.10)

The importance and interconnection of these two concepts—increasing text complexity and structuring the scaffolding of text complexity expectations by grade level—will assist students in becoming engaged, independent, active learners who are positioned to authentically interact with the knowledge and skills necessary for future success in the world.

All of our present and future students will need to possess robust content knowledge in order to become quality producers—in school and in their careers. As complex problem-solvers, students will need to value and use evidence. To be effective communicators, students will need to demonstrate the ability to read complex text independently, comprehend and respond to a wide range of topics, and critique and challenge/debate deeply with intensity and passion.

Text complexity is a topic that permeates all areas of instruction. Content-area teachers should ensure that resources for lessons, projects, readings, extended texts, short texts, and text passages are reflective of complexity levels appropriate for "on-grade-level" expectations and beyond. The topic, style, vocabulary, and purpose should all add to the value of the text planned for study.

For complex text to become a reality in classrooms, students need ongoing practice and contact with text samples. The text, through the accompanying lessons prepared by teachers, needs focus on developing student comprehension skills before, during, and after reading. The lessons need to demonstrate alignment with predetermined standards, be developmental in structure to scaffold learning for students, and always utilize formative assessment practices to gather evidence of student performance and progress.

Formative assessment is a process and utilizes multiple measures to monitor student progress and learning. It provides organic, ongoing feedback that can be used to inform teachers' instruction and assist students in improving their performance. Alternatively, summative assessments are instruments that evaluate student learning at the end of an instructional period by comparing student performance against a defined standard.

The Classroom:
10 Practical Strategies on Text Complexity

Keeping in mind the goal of students being able to independently read, comprehend, analyze, and evaluate complex texts, these strategies provide teachers with suggested ideas for implementation. The goal is for students to develop improved higher-order thinking skills and abilities so that they can use reasoning to communicate and interpret information accurately and effectively. Students should be able to demonstrate and expand their knowledge through discovering the author's purpose, expressing main ideas, discussing key points, and asking relevant questions.

When considering which complex texts to use in the instructional process, acceptable texts include print, digital (audio, visual, graphic), and online reference materials.

1. Hold students to higher expectations. Do not underestimate students' abilities to do better, especially in becoming better readers. Students possessing a wide range of background knowledge and diverse reading skills represent the reality that exists in most classrooms today. As teachers, our goal for all of our students is to have each of them attain the standard of reading at or above grade level. To make this goal a reality, educators need to consider a span of grade-level complex texts for the full range of students.

Increasing the level of rigor of the texts, exposing students to grade-level selections that incrementally escalate, and providing scaffolded instruction that students need to understand the text is where this process begins. Scaffolding continues over time but is changed or withdrawn as students' proficiency develops and they can sustain independence. As students increase proficiency levels, scaffolding escalates to support the challenges of the new levels. For students who are reading at advanced levels (e.g., above grade level), diverse, challenging texts that provide acceleration and enrichment are required to meet students' needs and should be included in the instructional plan to stretch students' capabilities.

According to Fisher, Frey, and Lapp (2012), "As Bruner (1964), Vygotsky (1962), and every classroom teacher knows, with appropriately scaffolded instruction that is indeed based on continuous teacher assessment of the increasing bank of knowledge and language that a student has on a topic being studied, a student can learn to read texts that are beyond his or her instructional level and hopefully learn how to support his or her own reading of difficult text when the teacher is no longer at the reader's side" (p. 7).

2. Think about text complexity when planning and implementing lessons. Strategically incorporate complex texts as part of the curriculum and instruction plan/program to allow reading opportunities in accordance with the prescribed or required curriculum/instructional framework. Purposefully planning the use of complex texts allows for the scaffolding of the selected texts so that integrated instructional units can build through increasingly expanding topics/themes, contrasting views, and multilayered, performance-based assignments. The body of information and knowledge dealt with in a text must be carefully thought out at three levels: the lesson, the grade-level curriculum, and the spectrum of K–12 curriculum goals.

An example of this would be that students should be expected to study a topic for a sustained period of time (e.g., unit of study), reading multiple texts/titles so that they gather depth of information on the topic. The units of study could be connected through the grades, with students gaining deeper understanding of the topic as they continuously study the topic. There would be an easy fit if the units of study were based in the content areas (e.g., science or history/social studies, etc.). This integrated unit approach would encourage teachers across content areas to collaborate in their planning and delivery of instructional units. The activities and readings would be coordinated and enable students to connect learning across subjects. This integration is critical at all grade levels as it makes learning more meaningful.

A specific example of an integrated unit based in science instruction would have students study the human body and connect it to English language arts/literacy through the readings they do. At the early grade levels (kindergarten and first), students would study how to take care of their body and read grade-level informational texts on hygiene, exercise, healthy eating, etc. In the next grade level (second), students would explore the human body again but at a more comprehensive level. They would study how the body works and read grade-level technical texts that show how basic body systems work. They would continue to study how to take care of their bodies by learning about diseases, preventing illnesses, germs, etc. In the subsequent grades (third and fourth), students would once again study the human body but focus more deeply on each of the body systems and research such systems as the circulatory system, the digestive system, the respiratory system, the muscular system, etc. Students would read multiple sources on the same subject so that they could understand the concept of research and compare the topic across sources. Each time students are involved with the unit of study on the human body, they expand their learning and develop more technical knowledge. (Common Core State Standards for English Language Arts in History/Social Studies, Science, and Technical Subjects, p. 33)

3. Spotlight key structural elements of nonfiction genres. Informational text is complicated because of its varied purposes. The purpose dictates the structure of the text. Not all informational texts have the same structure. Since nonfiction encompasses several well-defined genres (narrative, informational, expository, technical, and persuasive) and they each have distinct purposes, structures, and literary elements, it is important for teachers to provide explicit instruction for students in what each type looks like and what the structural elements are. Students should be afforded frequent and ample opportunities to view, interact with, and practice each of the genres, the purposes, and their structural and literary elements so that they become familiar and easily recognizable.

4. Teach the attributes of complex text. Complex text elements need to be identified and focused on during the instructional process. Students should become proficient in recognizing the elements that make the text complex. Focus on these important qualitative basics (Student Achievement Partners, 2013):

- subtle and/or frequent transitions
- multiple and/or subtle themes and purposes
- density of information
- unfamiliar settings, topics, or events
- lack of repetition
- overlap or similarity in words and sentences
- complex sentences
- uncommon vocabulary
- lack of words, sentences, or paragraphs that review or pull things together for the student
- longer paragraphs

5. Draw on anchor texts to guide practice. An anchor text is a text related to a unit or lesson. Teachers can read these with students and use them repeatedly to model reading the text for different purposes. An anchor text can be a book, a news article, a chapter (or part of one) from a novel, a biography, or an autobiography. Anchor texts can be drawn from books about history, social studies, science, and the arts as well as from technical texts, including directions, forms, and information displayed in graphs, charts, or maps.

In most cases, an anchor text is a short piece that is used frequently and is accompanied by concise lessons that focus on the elemental skills students need to practice and internalize to improve reading achievement. Teachers use the anchor text as a tool to work on comprehension strategies. Because the text is used many times, students become accustomed to the text and can concentrate on the skill(s) the teacher has selected for deep study. A detailed list of comprehension skills that the teacher could focus on before, during, and after the multiple readings appears on page 17.

6. Make the most of read-alouds. Students at all grade levels can derive many benefits from read-alouds and listening to audio recordings of books, texts, etc. Research tells us that reading aloud is fundamental for literacy development. Back in 1985, *Becoming a Nation of Readers: The Report of the Commission on Reading* stated that "The single most important activity for building the knowledge required for eventual success in reading is reading aloud to children" (p. 23). The report further elaborated that "There is no substitute for a teacher who reads children good stories. It whets the appetite of children for reading, and provides a model of skillful oral reading. It is a practice that should continue throughout the grades" (p. 51).

Throughout the ages, reading aloud has been the time-trusted strategy to improve students' love of reading. In the past, elders read aloud to youngsters to pass along information, lore, and family histories. In current times, parents and grandparents read fiction and nonfiction books based on a child's age and interests at bedtime. Additionally, many adults regularly listen to narrated books. Read-alouds cement the connection between the printed word and the meaning of the text.

In the classroom setting, a read-aloud is the oral reading of a book or passage connected to the theme of a unit or lesson topic. Read-alouds are used to strengthen students' understanding by developing background knowledge, increasing comprehension skills, and promoting critical thinking. Read-alouds also cultivate students' listening skills. Fountas and Pinnell (1996) tell us that "Children can listen on a higher language level than they can read, so reading aloud makes complex ideas more accessible and exposes children to vocabulary and language patterns that are not part of everyday speech." This helps students better understand what they read and builds independence in comprehension.

It is an established best practice to have students practice reading aloud. Reading aloud forces students to slow down while reading. Typically, reading more slowly aids in comprehension, as the reader has more time to process what he or she is reading. Reading aloud allows students to make a more intentional and thoughtful connection between the written words on the page and the same words spoken aloud.

7. Identify and analyze information from text features. There are visual cues and signals included in the way text is organized. These indicators are provided by the author to denote and emphasize information of substance and value with the text. Headings, subheadings, captions, indices, charts, sidebars, bold and italicized text, visuals, and diagrams are common text features that provide meaningful cues related to the text. These features are important and contribute to the readers' understanding of the text.

Explaining how students can examine the text for indicators of importance and demonstrating how students can analyze and evaluate information from text features are skills needed when engaging with complex text. Guiding students in previewing the chapter and formulating a topical outline using the text features is a prereading strategy that contributes to increased reading comprehension.

8. Coach students to read like detectives. When proficient readers interact with text, they read in a fashion similar to a good detective trying to solve a case. They read *into* the text and look for clues and hints pointing to what the author is describing or providing information about. Students also engage in an internal dialogue with the author as they are reading to try to understand the author's purpose, key ideas, traits of the characters, etc.

Using problem-solving strategies and clarifying questions as the students interact with the text helps them use text-based evidence to better comprehend what they are reading and draw conclusions from the text. These strategies require an understanding that extends beyond recalling basic facts and often require students to make inferences from what they have read.

Here are a few sample questions that can help students discover meaning:

- Why does the author…?
- Why is the title a good title for this selection? Explain using evidence.
- Who are the main characters? Justify your answer with evidence from the text.
- What is the main idea of the selection? Provide evidence to support your answer.
- Which character changes throughout the selection? Identify the character and tell how the character changes. Cite evidence from the text.
- What are the key details? Summarize and give evidence to explain why these are the most important details.

There are many resources online that provide text-dependent question stems and frames aligned to literature types and the CCSS College and Career Readiness Standards for Reading. Searching online for "text-dependent question stems and frames" brings up sources from school districts that have developed and used these formats as structures to support students' reading development in the elementary, middle, and secondary grades. Try some of them with students!

9. Keep a reading notebook. Taking notes is a tried-and-true method for supporting reading comprehension. As they begin this process, students may need instruction and modeling so that they can practice their note-taking skills. They will need to be instructed on specifics to record and how notes might be arranged: narrative sentences, lists, charts, etc. Generally, as the process progresses, students can be encouraged to construct their own notes based on their needs. Some students may need to take occasional notes while others may need a more scripted approach.

Students should record what they recall about each chapter or section of the text. Sometimes notes may even recall events at the paragraph level. Students should summarize the important points so that their notes are reflective of the essence of the text, the chronology of events, major events, significant problems/challenges, all characters as they are introduced and their relationships, etc.

Students should be able to retell the "story" of the text by reviewing their notes, which highlight all of the significant occurrences in the text, spotlighting the characters and discussing the problem/issue. Students should be able to offer supporting reasons from the text and hypothesize potential solutions based on what they read.

10. Champion independent reading. Having students become independent readers is a primary goal of teachers at every grade level. Independent reading can be part of the school-day literacy program and also be conducted beyond the school walls. The goal of a robust independent reading program is to invite students to read more every day. It supports the idea of students choosing to read on their own and voluntarily. The material to be read is a personal choice from a wide variety of sources for the purpose of gaining information and for enjoyment and pleasure.

Students are provided the opportunity to self-select and read books in which they are interested and able to comprehend at their "just-right" reading level. Since students have taken the control of what they can read, their confidence is boosted and they embody motivation and enthusiasm, all of which contribute to improved accuracy and success as readers. Independent reading sets students on the path for becoming enthusiastic lifelong readers, not simply readers of school material.

Teachers can strengthen independent reading by encouraging students to navigate, incrementally, more complex texts and accelerate achievement over time. Creating a vibrant independent reading program involves building a classroom library with interesting, exciting, and learning-forward books from various genres and reading levels being available for daily reading. Students should be able to take books home for independent reading time, which should be expected to be sustained for 15–45 minutes daily, depending on the students' level.

Students can easily increase their volume of reading and read more widely by reading digital text. Teachers can provide guidance to accessing online sites that provide free online content, including media content.

Online Resources for Extending Learning

It is a challenge for teachers to supplement their resources with new text-complexity materials that will interest students and engage them in rich, topic-specific content passages—both literary and informational. There are a number of online sources that provide educators with published materials and digital resources that are free, downloadable, and sources of text across content areas.

- American Memory Project—The Library of Congress offers teachers classroom materials and professional development resources to assist them in effectively using primary sources from the library's extensive digital collections in their teaching.
- Colorín Colorado—A bilingual website for educators with resources to help ELL students become successful lifelong readers.
- Discovery Kids—A collection of videos on a range of science-focused topics.

- The History Channel Classroom—Features television programs that teachers can record and keep for up to one year; provides support materials for lesson plans and class activities; and hosts a repository of historical speeches and videos.
- International Children's Digital Library—High-quality digital books from around the world.
- National Geographic Kids—Articles and videos on trending topics including environment and conservation, science and technology, people and culture, energy, archaeology, etc.
- NeoK12—Offers video clips and lessons for grades K–12 in ELA, math, science, social studies, and health.
- The Learning Network: Teaching and Learning with *The New York Times*— Categorized suggestions for informational text read-alouds from *Times'* essays, articles, op-eds, and humor pieces on a range of topics for students at all grade levels.
- Poetry 180—This site features poems selected by Billy Collins, former Poet Laureate of the United States, and offers students the opportunity to hear or read a poem each day of the school year.
- Smithsonian Tween Tribune—Daily news sites that offer a range of compelling, relevant, and interesting news articles from animals to science for young students, tweens, and teens.
- Time for Kids—Current event news articles, video clips, and informational text printables on various topics for all grade levels.

Summary

Successfully reading and understanding complex texts in literature and in nonfiction (high-quality informational texts) are skills that are central to the claims proffered on the summative ELA assessments aligned to national and/or state standards. In order to perform acceptably on the assessments, students will need to be prepared in advance through effective classroom experiences. They need to engage in reading a range of genres while teachers explicitly teach comprehension strategies via modeling and providing guided practice appropriate for various genres and for a variety of purposes. As teachers, we are the best reading role models.

Since the assessments will be utilizing multimodal formats (e.g., print texts and other media texts), this chapter provided congruent strategies for teachers to incorporate into lessons designed to foster comprehension of discipline-specific texts. The chapter also focused on coherence across the curriculum fostered through interdisciplinary collaboration between teachers and intertextual connections between texts in terms of subject matter, topics, themes, issues, and genre elements.

CHAPTER 2:
Close Reading, Using Evidence from a Text, and Text-Dependent Questions

Chapter 1 introduced the concepts of reading comprehension and text complexity. It elaborated on the importance of students reading grade-level complex text—both literary and informational—and doing it proficiently and independently. Building capacity with reading skills, such as defining words as they are used in context, interpreting the meaning of phrases, analyzing text structures, and understanding and discussing the author's purpose, can only be developed through practice. Allam (2012) explains that to "ensure our students are college and career ready, we must teach them critical reading strategies in order for them to independently attack a text. They must learn how to own a text, rather than letting the text own them."

Close reading, using evidence from a text, and text-dependent questions are instructional approaches that elementary teachers can incorporate into their bank of literacy best practices to intensify students' comprehension of complex text. Through meaningful instruction, teachers strive to develop students' thinking about reading and how they can relate to a text's important ideas by reading for a purpose and comprehending what an author has to say on a given subject. At all grade levels, beginning in elementary school, students are expected to converse about the author's words, discern the meaning of his/her message, and be able to understand and analyze the author's purpose. After having read the text, and after much examination, discussion, and internalization, students should then be able to use their own words, ideas, and experiences to construct their own representative version while expressing the author's intended meaning.

This chapter opens by centralizing our thinking on the close reading approach and provides information on how to implement strategies that will build capacity for both teachers and students. Attributes of close reading implementation are detailed. Next, the chapter concentrates on the importance of citing textual evidence and looks at standards across grade levels, highlighting the expected performance required from students.

The chapter elaborates on practical and useful classroom strategies for teachers to draw on when conducting close reading lessons and developing and using text-dependent questions. These strategies can be added to teachers' catalogs of reliable activities for helping students develop awareness, familiarity, and proficiency with asking and answering text-dependent questions.

Summative Assessments: What to Expect

Two Assessment Components

The summative ELA assessments, developed to measure the implementation of national and state standards, are designed to include a performance ELA assessment and a year-end ELA assessment. Both components differ in intent, format, and the products they expect students to complete. At the time that this book went to print, the two parts were administered at distinct time periods in the spring.

The two-part administration cycle means that in the typical configuration of a 10-month school year (August/May or September/June), the ELA performance assessment is administered at a time point approximately 75 percent through the school year. The second assessment, the ELA year-end assessment, is administered at a time point approximately 90 percent through the school year.

The proposed score-reporting process combines students' performance on the ELA performance assessment with their performance on the ELA year-end assessment. One summative score report for the student in ELA/literacy is released, with detailed results on several levels.

The main reason that the assessments are scheduled at the two different time points is that students will be required to produce extended written responses (essays, etc.) that may need to be scored by human scorers, which takes additional time. The responses on the ELA year-end assessment are question/answer-type responses, which can be machine scored.

As this book went to print, the summative ELA assessments have being completed by millions of students across many states. The designers and producers of the commercially available summative ELA assessments have sought detailed feedback on the initial administration from key state and district stakeholders to refine and improve the tests. This continuous improvement and enhancement of their products is resulting in changes for future administrations. Proposed changes are currently being announced. The changes are designed to simplify the design without diminishing the goal of the assessment and shorten the administration time frames.

Moving forward, the goal is to offer a comprehensive summative ELA assessment during one condensed test administration window. For example, in the typical configuration of a 10-month school year (August/May or September/June), the improved summative ELA will be comprehensive and include the performance assessment. It will be administered at a single time point between 75–90 percent through the school year.

The improved summative ELA assessment design also seeks to reduce the total ELA testing time for students along with reducing the number of ELA assessment scenarios and accompanying questions.

Focus on Close Reading—Text Passages

For students at each grade level, summative ELA assessments in reading are being carefully constructed to assess comprehension and reasoning skills through reading sufficiently complex and challenging passages in a wide array of subject areas. The reading passages that students will encounter are authentic literary and informational texts worthy of study and have been selected from quality published sources. In some cases, on some assessments, passages have been constructed specifically for the assessment.

On the assessments, text passages will represent an array of literary genres (fiction, poetry, and drama) and informational text types (literary nonfiction, historical, and science and technical). The content will span historical time periods and encompass world cultures. Text passages will also be extracted from U.S. founding documents (e.g., the Pledge of Allegiance, the Declaration of Independence, the Constitution, or the Bill of Rights) appropriate to the grade level. Historical texts could include primary source selections by Abraham Lincoln, John F. Kennedy, or Martin Luther King Jr., as well as from an author writing on a topic such as choice, freedom, or independence.

Multimedia passages (video and audio clips, podcasts, websites, etc.) are included as sources of text. These sources will complement the written passages at all grade levels. Students, beginning in grade three, will be presented with paired text passages and combinations of text and multimedia formats.

In summary, success on the newly redesigned summative ELA assessments given in grades three through eight now focus on students' knowledge and skill in reading passages and responding to various question types by:

- synthesizing information from different portions of passages or entire texts;
- paraphrasing statements as they are used in the text;
- drawing conclusions about the main characters in challenging literary or nonfiction narratives;
- identifying or inferring a central idea or theme in complex passages or their paragraphs; and
- summarizing key supporting ideas and details in complex passages.

Through the development of close reading strategies, students will be better able to demonstrate their knowledge, skills, and understanding and be able to apply their expertise to problems and concepts steeped in science, social studies, health, the arts, and career-related technical contexts.

Focus on Evidence from a Text

The summative ELA assessments aligned to national and/or state standards propel student learning to a deeper level beyond minimally identifying and locating basic facts (e.g., names, dates, events) in a reading passage. Students must show a better grasp of and expertise with textual evidence. The assessments consistently address students' skillfulness to understand and use evidence in reading in a wide range of subjects and contexts, including literature and literary nonfiction, history/social studies, science, and career-related technical texts and topics.

Students will be expected to jockey between the text, or multiple texts, and the questions following the passages to locate and select the best answers to the multistep and multidimensional questions being put forth. Frequently, in a hefty quantity of the questions, there are two question sequences that pertain to the same information. In the first question, students are asked for the correct selected response. In the second question—which extends the thinking related to the first response—students are asked to select one or more segments (e.g., sentences, paragraphs) from the text that serve as the best evidence to support their answer to the first question. In this two-part question series, scoring is based providing correct answers to both questions. On paper-based assessments, this is a tricky task; however, now that most students will be taking the assessments online, the challenge is heightened as students will need to manipulate both the texts and the questions on screen simultaneously.

Students will also be required to ascertain the meaning of words and phrases in the context of the passages and determine how word choice shapes meaning, tone, and impact. There will be two-part vocabulary-based questions with the accompanying second question entailing the student provide evidence of contextual use.

The goals for each grade level are for students to thoroughly interact with texts, be able to interpret details and draw logical conclusions from information presented in complex passages, and supply correct answers to the questions following each passage on the summative assessment.

Focus on Text-Dependent Questions

Summative ELA assessments will rely heavily on the use of text-dependent questions. It is through evidence-based responses to text-dependent questions that students will demonstrate their skills and abilities to read carefully and deeply and use specific evidence from complex texts to obtain and defend correct responses. Several text-dependent questions will follow each of the texts or multimedia passages so that students can demonstrate their understanding of each text explicitly. In most cases, question types on the summative ELA assessments will consist of a two-question format requiring that students select more than one evidence statement in response to the accompanying selected response question.

In order to be successful on summative ELA assessments, high-quality instruction must occur daily and formative assessment practices need to be in place. The goal is for teachers to formatively and continuously assess student performance as part of the instructional cycle to ensure that students' needs are being met and that students are sustaining learning at an independent level over the course of a school year and beyond. Instructional practices during the literacy block and across content-area subjects rely on sophisticated strategies, such as close reading, as they will be utilized through high school and college courses. Close reading, as an instructional approach or routine, has been in place for many years. Let's take a look at how we can leverage this highly developed methodology to our advantage in meeting the needs of our students and supporting their path to higher achievement and future success.

What Is Close Reading?

There are many variations of definitions of close reading. All of them contribute to a complete understanding of the concept and provide insight into its instructional underpinnings. According to Fisher and Frey (2012), "close reading is an instructional routine in which students critically examine a text, especially through repeated readings" (p. 179).

McClennen (2001), in "Dr. McClennen's Close Reading Guide: How to Do a Close Reading," explains what it means to read closely. She describes it as: "…developing a deep understanding and a precise interpretation of a literary passage that is based first and foremost on the words themselves. But a close reading does not stop there; rather, it embraces larger themes and ideas evoked and/or implied by the passage itself."

Brown and Kappes (2012) provide a definition that is more explicit and structured: "Close reading of text involves an investigation of a short piece of text, with multiple readings done over multiple instructional lessons. Through text-based questions and discussion, students are guided to deeply analyze and appreciate various aspects of the text, such as key vocabulary and how its meaning is shaped by context; attention to form, tone, imagery and/or rhetorical devices; the significance of word choice and syntax; and the discovery of different levels of meaning as passages are read multiple times" (p. 2).

In her article, "Closing in on Close Reading," Boyles (2012) provides an overarching definition: "Essentially, close reading means reading to uncover layers of meaning that lead to deep comprehension" (p. 36).

These definitions help us, as practitioners, visualize the instructional planning, teaching processes, and formative assessment strategies that need to be provided for students to learn these skills explicitly and directly. There are common fundamental elements that structurally define the process of close reading instruction (Fisher and Frey, 2012; Boyles, 2012; Brown and Kappes, 2012). A synopsis of the process steps is delineated here:

1. Choose and use a short, meaningful complex text of superior quality.
2. Limit "front-loading" (Fisher and Frey, 2012, p. 181); curtail prereading of the text.
3. Have the teacher model the reading of the text while students follow along.
4. Direct instruction by reading the selection multiple times—at least three—for different purposes (engages students in connecting with the text).
   a. Read the text independently for comprehension.
   b. Read for different purposes—focus on the author's word choices, recurring themes, and literary devices.
   c. Read with a pencil (Fisher and Frey, 2012, p. 186) and annotate to check understanding.
5. Conduct teacher-led shared reading and think-alouds.
   a. Use text-based questions to solicit responses of subtle details, characterizations, author's meaning, etc. from the text.
6. Use a writing assignment as a follow-up culminating activity to the close reading session.

Designing instruction so that students frequently and actively participate in close reading experiences provides them with opportunities to apply the new skills and strategies they are learning and strengthen their understanding of texts that are complex, challenging, and, in most cases, above their independent reading levels. Not every text is a candidate for a close reading experience. Texts must be carefully selected and aligned with purposeful instruction. The close reading scenario is designed to consume multiple segments or class sessions; however, the investment of time is only surpassed by the progress in student learning outcomes and the gains in student performance.

Close Reading Learning Outcomes

The goal of close reading is for students to become independent and discerning readers and writers, but we want them also to become complex and critical thinkers. Close reading follows the gradual release of responsibility model in which we, as teachers, move students from a teacher-directed environment to one in which the students employ and sustain the strategies on their own...independently (Brown and Kappes, 2012). We want them to transfer their learning. According to Boyles (2012), "the goal is for students to take what they learn from the study of one text and apply it to the next text they read" (p. 40). We want them to apply their knowledge in new and novel situations, using the skills they have learned.

Boyles (2012) suggests students keep these four basic questions as a guide when reflecting on a specific portion of any text—even short, brief passages:

- What is the author *telling* me here?
- Are there any hard or important *words*?
- What does the author want me to *understand*?
- How does the author play with *language* to add to meaning? (p. 40)

In the quest to become independent readers, students will need a great deal of persistence on the part of teachers. Teachers must delve in with students to uncover multiple levels of meaning associated with the four questions above. Teachers need to continue to use probing text-dependent questions that relate to important aspects and understandings of the text and the author's intention and reasoning.

Text Evidence in Reading, Writing, and Speaking

The Common Core State Standards brought reading closely, citing evidence from the text, and asking/answering text-dependent questions to the forefront of the professional conversations and work involving instructional supervisors, curriculum writers (usually teachers), classroom teachers, students, parents, and publishers. In the past, these instructional methods were integrated into various English language arts/literacy programs, some classroom practices, and some teachers' instructional toolboxes. Presently, there appears to be a critical need to revisit existing practices and escalate close reading, using evidence from the text and text-dependent questions to the apex of implementation across all classrooms, not just the English language arts/literacy class.

Common Core Reading Standard 1 provides a vertical progression of complexity through the grades. Student skill development related to reading closely, examining texts, citing evidence, and making logical inferences is structured as grade-by-grade requisites for increasing students' proficiency and independence.

The standards place prime emphasis on the skill of reading closely as well as students' interactions with the text. The expectation for students in all grades is to read, write, and speak grounded in evidence from the text, beginning in kindergarten and continuing through grade 12. In keeping with the book's purpose, the following chart highlights the specifications for grade levels three through eight.

The grade-specific standards for College and Career Readiness (CCR) Anchor Reading Standard 1 are represented by the same descriptions for both literary text (RL) and informational text (RI). They are represented in this combined chart.

Reading: Literature and Informational Text

Source: Common Core State Standards (2010)

CCR Anchor Standard 1: Read closely to determine what the text says explicitly and to make logical inferences from it; cite specific textual evidence when writing or speaking to support conclusions drawn from the text.

Grade	Grade-Specific Standard
Grade 3	Ask and answer questions to demonstrate understanding of a text, referring explicitly to the text as the basis for the answers. (CCSS.ELA-Literacy.RL.3.1 and CCSS.ELA-Literacy.RI.3.1)
Grade 4	Refer to details and examples in a text when explaining what the text says explicitly and when drawing inferences from the text. (CCSS.ELA-Literacy.RL.4.1 and CCSS.ELA-Literacy.RI.4.1)
Grade 5	Quote accurately from a text when explaining what the text says explicitly and when drawing inferences from the text. (CCSS.ELA-Literacy.RL.5.1 and CCSS.ELA-Literacy.RI.5.1)
Grade 6	Cite textual evidence to support analysis of what the text says explicitly as well as inferences drawn from the text. (CCSS.ELA-Literacy.RL.6.1 and CCSS.ELA-Literacy.RI.6.1)
Grade 7	Cite several pieces of textual evidence to support analysis of what the text says explicitly as well as inferences drawn from the text. (CCSS.ELA-Literacy.RL.7.1 and CCSS.ELA-Literacy.RI.7.1)
Grade 8	Cite the textual evidence that most strongly supports an analysis of what the text says explicitly as well as inferences drawn from the text. (CCSS.ELA-Literacy.RL.8.1 and CCSS.ELA-Literacy.RI.8.1)

CCR Reading Standard 1 is the pillar standard at each grade level; however, it is supported by the other nine CCR standards as grade-level indicators students need to master. Here is an overview of the standards needing mastery at the eighth-grade level:

CCSS Reading Standards: Grade 8	
Source: Common Core State Standards (2010)	
LITERATURE	**INFORMATIONAL TEXT**
Key Ideas and Details	
CCSS.ELA-Literacy.RL.8.1: Cite the textual evidence that most strongly supports an analysis of what the text says explicitly as well as inferences drawn from the text.	CCSS.ELA-Literacy.RI.8.1: Cite the textual evidence that most strongly supports an analysis of what the text says explicitly as well as inferences drawn from the text.
CCSS.ELA-Literacy.RL.8.2: Determine a theme or central idea of a text and analyze its development over the course of the text, including its relationship to the characters, setting, and plot; provide an objective summary of the text.	CCSS.ELA-Literacy.RI.8.2: Determine a central idea of a text and analyze its development over the course of the text, including its relationship to supporting ideas; provide an objective summary of the text.
CCSS.ELA-Literacy.RL.8.3: Analyze how particular lines of dialogue or incidents in a story or drama propel the action, reveal aspects of a character, or provoke a decision.	CCSS.ELA-Literacy.RI.8.3: Analyze how a text makes connections among and distinctions between individuals, ideas, or events (e.g., through comparisons, analogies, or categories).
Craft and Structure	
CCSS.ELA-Literacy.RL.8.4: Determine the meaning of words and phrases as they are used in a text, including figurative and connotative meanings; analyze the impact of specific word choices on meaning and tone, including analogies or allusions to other texts.	CCSS.ELA-Literacy.RI.8.4: Determine the meaning of words and phrases as they are used in a text, including figurative, connotative, and technical meanings; analyze the impact of specific word choices on meaning and tone, including analogies or allusions to other texts.
CCSS.ELA-Literacy.RL.8.5: Compare and contrast the structure of two or more texts and analyze how the differing structure of each text contributes to its meaning and style.	CCSS.ELA-Literacy.RI.8.5: Analyze in detail the structure of a specific paragraph in a text, including the role of particular sentences in developing and refining a key concept.

-continued

CCSS Reading Standards: Grade 8

Source: Common Core State Standards (2010)

LITERATURE	INFORMATIONAL TEXT
CCSS.ELA-Literacy.RL.8.6: Analyze how differences in the points of view of the characters and the audience or reader (e.g., created through the use of dramatic irony) create such effects as suspense or humor.	CCSS.ELA-Literacy.RI.8.6: Determine an author's point of view or purpose in a text and analyze how the author acknowledges and responds to conflicting evidence or viewpoints.
Integration of Knowledge and Ideas	
CCSS.ELA-Literacy.RL.8.7: Analyze the extent to which a filmed or live production of a story or drama stays faithful to or departs from the text or script, evaluating the choices made by the director or actors.	CCSS.ELA-Literacy.RI.8.7: Determine an author's point of view or purpose in a text and analyze how the author acknowledges and responds to conflicting evidence or viewpoints.
CCSS.ELA-Literacy.RL.8.8: (Not applicable for literature.)	CCSS.ELA-Literacy.RI.8.8: Delineate and evaluate the argument and specific claims in a text, assessing whether the reasoning is sound and the evidence is relevant and sufficient; recognize when irrelevant evidence is introduced.
CCSS.ELA-Literacy.RL.8.9: Analyze how a modern work of fiction draws on themes, patterns of events, or character types from myths, traditional stories, or religious works such as the Bible, including describing how the material is rendered new.	CCSS.ELA-Literacy.RI.8.9: Analyze a case in which two or more texts provide conflicting information on the same topic and identify where the texts disagree on matters of fact or interpretation.
Range of Reading and Level of Text Complexity	
CCSS.ELA-Literacy.RL.8.10: By the end of the year, read and comprehend literature, including stories, dramas, and poems, at the high end of grades 6–8 text complexity band independently and proficiently.	CCSS.ELA-Literacy.RI.8.10: By the end of the year, read and comprehend literary nonfiction at the high end of the grades 6–8 text complexity band independently and proficiently.

Constructing and Using Text-Dependent Questions

Close reading is a viable and worthy strategy and has a real value in classroom instruction. Just like anything else, it is worth the teacher's investment in learning how to implement this approach with zeal and knowledge. Text-dependent questions, as the name indicates, ask students to provide evidence from the text and draw inferences based on what the text says. Text-dependent questions that are artfully developed engage students in reflecting on the text and thinking critically beyond the words to the meaning of the thoughts and ideas being presented. Constructing text-dependent questions that are intentional and focused is a skill that teachers will need to practice in order to deepen their own understanding.

For far too long, both in classroom experiences (conversations, discussions, teacher-made tests, grade-level assessments) and on standardized assessments, many questions required no connection to the text being read or discussed. In many cases, the student could answer the question correctly and sufficiently without ever having read the text. Critical analysis requires skill-based questioning that is focused on wide-ranging facets permeating the text.

Well-crafted text-dependent questions ensure precise understanding of the text through an emphasis on key terms, use of words, phrasing, and subtleties that students would not have paid attention to in a quick read-through. According to Liben and Liben (2013), text-dependent questions ask students to carry out one or more of the following tasks (p. 1):

- Analyze paragraphs on a sentence-by-sentence basis and sentences on a word-by-word basis to determine the role played by individual paragraphs, sentences, phrases, or words

- Investigate how meaning can be altered by changing key words and why an author may have chosen one word over another

- Probe each argument in persuasive text, each idea in informational text, each key detail in literary text, and observe how these build to a whole

- Examine how shifts in the direction of an argument or explanation are achieved and the impact of those shifts

- Question why authors choose to begin and end when they do

- Note and assess patterns of writing and what they achieve

- Consider what the text leaves uncertain or unstated

It is important to remember that text-dependent questions always keep the text as the primary focus and all of the questions are geared to important aspects of the text. Focusing on what is essential will help students retain it and consider important elements when reading future texts.

The Classroom: 10 Practical Strategies on Close Reading and Text-Dependent Questions

1. Select the right text for close reading. Choose a text that is more challenging than texts students are presently reading during literacy instruction. Consider what would be of grade-level complexity to correspond to the level at which they should be reading to achieve proficiency. The passage should be at the upper level of the grade-level text complexity band and should stretch students' capabilities. The passage should be short but content rich and literacy dense.

Use the Lexile Analyzer on the Lexile.com website to establish the Lexile level of the text passage. The selected text can be cut and pasted directly into the analyzer, or you can browse for saved files and select one for placement into the analyzer. Once the text is submitted, the Lexile rank and corresponding helpful information appear on the screen.

After selecting the text, begin to develop corresponding text-dependent questions. The text-dependent questions should require students to think more deeply each time they reread the selected text. Using class data gathered through ongoing formative assessments, focus the questions on a skill or strategy that students need more assistance in mastering or should be using more consistently. The questions could focus on author's message and craft, key ideas and details, and integration of knowledge and ideas.

2. Number the paragraphs in a text passage. This strategy may seem very simple and straightforward. Having students number the paragraphs (usually in the left margin directly next to the first word in the paragraph) helps them organize their thoughts, prepares them to cite evidence from a specific location, and provides a structure for note-taking. Depending on the length of the passage, this can be a helpful hint for preparing students for the summative ELA assessments as most commercially-produced assessments present passages that are numbered. Numbering provides a referencing system for questions for which students must provide responses.

3. Turn every reader into a close rereader. Incorporate close reading lessons into the instructional schedule on a regular basis so that students participate in ample opportunities to practice and develop the necessary skills. Have students participate in multiple and purposeful rereadings of the identified text(s). Students should reread a text at least three times. Each time the passage is reread, students should be digging deeper into the text to get to the bedrock of the author's purpose and uncover intricacies about vocabulary, voice, meaning, and structure.

Through developing question stems and question prompts that can be categorized and practiced, students will become more adept and efficient. According to Fisher (2012), rereading a text is "an encounter where students really focus on what the author had to say, what the author's purpose was, what the words mean, and what the structure of the text tells us."

4. Access the Basal Alignment Project and Anthology Alignment Project for free lesson plans with text-dependent questions. The Council of the Great City Schools and Student Achievement Partners partnered to launch two initiatives: the Basal Alignment Project (BAP) for grades three through five and the Anthology Alignment Project (AAP) for grades six through 10.

In the BAP, teacher teams were recruited to write text-dependent questions aligned to selections from popular reading/ELA textbooks. The teams evaluated existing questions embedded in the commercially available textbooks and accompanying resources. They focused on writing new, quality text-dependent questions to sources. Hundreds of teachers have worked collaboratively to develop these replacement materials, following intensive training on the Common Core by experts from the Student Achievement Partners.

Each replacement lesson has been authored, edited, and reviewed by a team of teachers. The new questions and lesson resources require students to read and respond to questions that require a closer reading of the text. More than 300 free, teacher-developed Common Core-aligned lessons for basal reading series in grades three through five are available to all teachers for download. These lessons can be used immediately in the classroom and for professional development. Teachers can link to Student Achievement Partners' achievethecore.org website and download and adapt materials for lesson planning and for use with students.

Similarly, for the Anthology Alignment Project, participants prepared lesson revisions, developed quality text-dependent questions, and improved tasks and culminating activities to support text selections. There was a strong focus on academic vocabulary. General education, English language learner, and special education teachers had an opportunity to collaborate on preparing CCSS-aligned, instructional classroom lessons for grades six through 10. These free, teacher-developed lessons can be downloaded from Student Achievement Partners' achievethecore.org website.

5. Stretch students' evidence searches through response stems. As students engage with text-dependent questions during close reading, there are ample opportunities for discussion to be incorporated during small-group and whole-class discussions. The teacher should shift the dynamic of the discussion so that students are doing most of the talking. The use of response stems can bridge students' statements to their next great thought and further develop and extend their last statement. In structuring dialogue between student partners, students can utilize the same response stems.

Expanding ideas:
- Allow me to take your statement one step further...
- Permit me to broaden your statement...
- You and I agree with each other, and therefore...

Expounding on the facts:
- Offer me a different instance where that occurred...
- Look back and find the words or sentences that are the basis of your opinion or statement...
- I don't understand. Clear up my confusion about...
- Give me more information to explain...
- Provide me with the evidence on how you made that inference...

Support your thinking:
- Elaborate on...
- Reveal more proof about...
- Reinforce your thinking by giving me more evidence on...
- Share the facts behind your thinking...

Countering the thinking:
- I don't share the same opinion about _____ because...
- I support the opposing point of view on _____ because...
- I disagree with the author about _____, and I can support my position with this evidence/these facts...
- My opinion conflicts with yours. Let me explain why...

6. Teach students to annotate the text. Instruct students to write on the text as they read it. Annotation includes underlining or highlighting key words and phrases—anything that strikes the reader as surprising or significant or that raises questions—as well as making notes in the margins. Students need to examine not just what is written but how it is written. Peculiar or unknown words, references, striking images, and points of view are recorded. Interacting with text in this way compels students to pay close attention.

7. Create serial readers. As students become more familiar with the components of close reading and text-dependent questions, there is an opportunity to transform them into serial readers—readers who read several texts (or books) on the same topic, across different genres. The goal is for students to read three or more texts on a topic. The volume of reading will naturally broaden their knowledge of a topic. By selecting texts (or books) representing varied genres, students will be better able to assess the various authors' viewpoints, reasoning, vocabulary use, and treatment of facts, etc. Reading several texts on the same topic will allow students to compare different versions of the same text, analyze how ideas are transformed from one text to another, and compare the structure of the texts. Becoming more critical readers will help them excel on summative ELA assessments in literacy. On the assessments, students will read several paired texts, be required to answer text-based questions based on each text, and make judgments that compare and contrast aspects of the texts.

8. Extend close reading with a culminating assignment. The culminating assignment needs to integrate the key understandings formulated for the close reading lesson and, in most cases, should involve writing. The assignment needs to be well crafted so that students can complete it independently. Remember that on the summative assessments, students will always write in response to having read one or more text passages or to having viewed a multimedia clip.

Here are examples of writing assignment tasks in prompt format:

The title of this selection is

_____

Using your answers from the questions, your notes, and class discussion, explain why this is an appropriate title for the selection. Be sure to clearly cite evidence from the text for each part of your answer.

We have read _____
                                        (text title)
and _____
                                        (text title)
Write an essay that analyzes the strength of the arguments about _____

_____
                      (attribute of character)

in at least two of the texts. Remember to use textual evidence from both texts to support your ideas.

9. Consider using Fisher and Frey's (2012) "Progression of Text-Dependent Questions." A taxonomy is the practice and science of orderly classification and giving names to the groups. When using a taxonomy, it is presumed that movement through the levels, or stages, begins at the lower levels and progresses up through the tiers, or layers, so that the skills associated with the highest levels can be accomplished successfully.

With intense focus on text-dependent questions, a new progression of question levels has been developed by Fisher and Frey (2012) that seeks to structure conceptual understanding of this topic. They have structured the progression into six categories of questions: "general understanding," "key details," "vocabulary and text structure," "author's purpose," "inferences," and "opinions, arguments, and inter-textual connections" (p. 73). Their taxonomy also considers how the questions broaden from being related to "part of the text to the whole text" (p. 73).

As educators develop and incorporate text-dependent questions into literacy experiences with the goal of moving students through the cognitive levels, they should think about using Fisher and Frey's six categories of questions. Their framework can be taken into account in order to develop progressively more complex text-dependent questions as their progression "moves from explicit to implicit in meaning and from sentence level to whole text and across multiple texts" (p. 73).

Teachers can determine which categories fit the selected text best and use this organizer as a reference when planning, writing, and using text-dependent questions. Depending on the grade level, teachers may think about introducing this organizer to students, encouraging them to develop text-dependent questions in addition to responding to them. Students in elementary and middle grades would clearly be capable of discerning the different categories, with teachers providing explicit instruction on how to use the "Progression of Text-Dependent Questions." Exemplar questions for each type could be developed.

Additionally, just like with any taxonomy, teachers can look at the kinds of text-dependent questions they are utilizing so that they can ensure a more comprehensive integration of the higher-level, implicit-type questions, allowing students to deepen their relationship with texts.

10. Assess potential instructional resource purchases. When considering the purchase of new instructional resources, be a critical consumer. If the goal is to purchase materials that support text-dependent questions, then thoroughly review the resource using the questions here. Conversely, the same set of questions can be used to assess the quality of question sets in materials that are already in use in the classroom.

Once this process is undertaken for previously purchased materials and prevailing gaps are identified, solutions can be formulated and fixes incorporated so that the issues can be corrected and eliminated.

Checklist for Evaluating Question Quality

Text Dependent (these items must be true of every question in the set):
- Does the student have to read the text to answer each question?
- Is it always clear to students that answering each question requires that they must use evidence from the text to support their claims? (CCSS 1 should always be in play.)

Text Specific
- Are the questions specific enough so they can only be answered by reference to this text?
- Are the inferences students are asked to make grounded logically in the text? (Can they be answered with careful reading rather than background knowledge?)

Organization of the Questions
- Do the early questions in the sequence focus on specific phrases and sentences to support basic comprehension of the text and develop student confidence before moving on to more challenging tasks?
- Are the questions coherently sequenced? Do they build toward gradual understanding of the text's meaning?
- Do the questions stay focused on the text and only go beyond it to make other connections in extension activities after the text has been explored?
- If multiple texts/different media are under consideration, are students asked to examine each text closely before making connections among texts?

-continued

Important Considerations

- At tricky or key points in the text, are there check-in questions for students to answer so that teachers can check on students' understanding and use these sections to enhance reading proficiency?

- Do questions provide an opportunity for students to determine the meaning of academic vocabulary in context? When possible, do some of these questions explore some aspect of the text as well as important vocabulary?

- Does the mix of questions addressing syntax, vocabulary, structure, and other inferences match the complexity of the text?

Culminating Activity or Writing Task

- Does the culminating task call on the knowledge and understanding acquired through the questions?

- Does the writing prompt in the culminating task demand that students write to the text and use evidence?

- Are the instructions to the teacher and the student clear about what must be performed to achieve proficiency?

- Is this a task worthy of the student and classroom time it will consume?

Adapted from Student Achievement Partners (2013)

Online Resources for Extending Learning

These online sites provide resources for teachers, including texts that can be used to expand teachers' collection of complex text passages used in ELA/literacy and content-area classrooms. The resources are free and downloadable.

- America in Class—Lessons from the National Humanities Center using primary resources. Provides background information and strategies that enable teachers and students to use close reading for the analysis of subject texts and images.

- ASCD—Association for Supervision and Curriculum Development offers online access to an extensive catalog of free resources that empower educators to support literacy success. *Educational Leadership*, its monthly online journal, provides up-to-date research and cutting-edge resources in professional development, capacity building, and educational leadership.

- Bartleby—Provides students with unlimited access to literature, references, and verse online, free of charge.

- Common Core State Standards Appendix B: Text Exemplars and Sample Performance Tasks—Text samples that serve to exemplify the level of complexity and quality that the standards require all students in a given grade band to engage with. Exemplar texts are provided for all grade levels and in all major content areas. Sample performance tasks are provided.

- International Literacy Association (formerly International Reading Association)—Publishes cutting-edge research on literacy and translates the research into practical resources for educators and students.

- The Lexile Framework for Reading/Lexile Analyzer—The Lexile Analyzer measures the complexity of the text by breaking down the uploaded text passage and studying its characteristics, such as sentence length and word frequency, which represent the syntactic and semantic challenges the text presents to a reader.

- Literacy for Life—The website of Drs. Douglas Fisher and Nancy Frey, literacy researchers and authors. In the "Publications" section, there are numerous journal articles on literacy concepts and strategies for teachers to use for professional learning purposes.

- Newsela—Newsela uses current events and daily news to build close reading and critical-thinking skills, giving students a new way to ascend the staircase of nonfiction reading comprehension, from fourth grade to college ready. Every article provided on the site has five reading levels. Newsela automatically gives each student the version of an article that's just right for his or her reading ability.

- Poetry for Kids—Children's Poet Laureate Kenn Nesbitt's site for funny poems and poetry books for students.

- ReadWorks—ReadWorks provides research-based units, lessons, and authentic, leveled nonfiction and literary passages directly to educators online, for free, to be shared broadly.

Summary

Chapter 2 delved into the concepts of close reading, using evidence from the text, and developing and using text-dependent questions to analyze both literature and informational texts. Through these targeted instructional practices, I am optimistic that we can captivate students with rich, authentic texts to become better readers who continuously develop deeper knowledge and skills through unprecedented experiences with texts.

The summative ELA assessments aligned to national and state standards are focused on grade-level reading. As students attend classes each day, they should be enthralled with what they read and mired in the quest to understand and unfold what the text means. What better way to make that happen than through a close reading experience with authentic text passages? School still provides us with the best opportunity to turn students into great readers for life. At each grade level, they should be voracious to learn new words, be keen to discover new worlds of provocative thought, and be animated in conversations and discussions about what they have read.

There is certainly room for students to have opinions about what they have read. Having a thorough understanding of the complexities of the text, coupled with stimulating conversations about what they have read, brings students to more informed opinions.

As a reader and as a teacher, I have always held the belief that it was my responsibility to exude a love of reading and encourage students to join the ranks of lifelong readers. Having taught the spectrum of students from first graders through students enrolled in master's and doctoral degree programs, I have been steadfast in that goal.

Now that we have seen what types of texts will comprise the summative ELA assessments aligned to national and/or state standards, it has renewed my expectations that students now have more need than ever to experience rich literature along with quality informational texts that extend learning. The sky's the limit in terms of what selections we choose!

CHAPTER 3:
Developing and Expanding Vocabulary

Words are important. They are essential to us as adults, but they are even more important to our students—students who are learning to read, write, and speak well. Words are more than just strings of letters connected in various configurations that students sound out or learn how to spell for a weekly review. Words have meaning for each of us. They are the essence of our conceptions, ideas, thoughts, sounds, and visual images. Words are the connective fibers that entwine our oral language encounters with written language experiences into the tapestry of our culture and our history. Stories, tales, songs, poetry, speeches, novels, informational guides, technical manuals, medical documents, architectural directions, historical essays, and so on, are all created by putting words together in a myriad of different patterns, tempos, and structures.

This chapter looks at the importance of developing students' vocabulary skills by increasing the number and kinds of words important for student success at their grade level and in their content-area subjects. Today, students are expected to be engaged readers, proficient writers, articulate speakers, and critical listeners who communicate through the use of eloquent, expressive, and operative words. A student's ability to read and understand words that progressively increase in complexity as they advance through school is a factor vital to school growth.

This chapter gives attention to developing an understanding and interest in words. It also concentrates on the importance of comprehensive and strong vocabulary work associated with literature and high-quality informational texts and how students will need to acquire deep understanding of the words through contextual clues and explicit learning.

Helpful classroom strategies are provided for teachers to draw on instructionally to build students' appreciation of words and their use, improve word-recognition skills, and develop word independence when interacting with complex text.

Summative Assessments: What to Expect

Focus on Vocabulary

The summative ELA assessments aligned to national and/or state standards for reading and writing focus keenly on vocabulary acquisition/development and application/use. This encompasses both the level and types of words students are expected to know and use in response to reading and writing tasks. The expectation for students performing successfully on the assessment tasks links directly to (1) increased student learning and (2) enhanced teaching through the development and implementation of a systematic approach to teaching vocabulary directly and also in context.

As the summative ELA assessments are administered during these initial upcoming years, teachers may find the level and type of words with which students will interact to be different, academically oriented, and challenging. Over time, as the assessments become more transparent based on items being released from the producers of the assessments, along with both teachers and students gearing their vocabulary work to best align with their standards-based curriculum, the rigor of the expected mastery will, hopefully, become routine and systematic.

Grade-level vocabulary collectively represents the words on the assessments. There will be vocabulary specific to the content of the ELA passages (literary and informational) and specific to the subject areas students are learning—science, social studies (history, geography, and civics), health, and the arts.

Words to Learn

It has been estimated that there are "1,025,109 words in the English language with a new word created every 98 minutes or about 14.7 words per day," according to the Global Language Monitor (2014). Furthermore, Nagy and Anderson's research (1984) validated that "printed school English, as represented by materials in grades 3 to 9, contains 88,533 distinct word families." There is no way that students will ever master the entirety of those words or word families, but students must develop fluency, accuracy, and automaticity with words as they progress through the grades.

According to Hirsch (2003), "A 12th-grade student who scores well enough on the verbal portion of the SAT to get into a selective college knows between 60,000 and 100,000 words. There is some dispute among experts regarding the actual number so we might split the difference and assume that the number is about 80,000" (p. 16). Every day, in every grade, there is a plethora of opportunities for students to learn new words through incidental means and explicit instruction and to connect those words into meaningful oral and written language in the form of sentences, paragraphs, stories, and essays.

The Importance of Vocabulary

Vocabulary refers to the body of words a student has learned and uses in different ways for different purposes. A synthesis of the research tells us that many students enter classrooms with their vocabulary limited by their experiences, background, and home environment. "Between grades 1 and 3, it is estimated that economically disadvantaged students' vocabularies increase by about 3,000 words per year and middle-class students' vocabularies increase by about 5,000 words per year" (University of Oregon's Center on Teaching and Learning, 2015).

Typically, a student's vocabulary increases with age, expands with interaction and communication, and deepens through the acquisition of new knowledge. "Children's vocabulary size approximately doubles between grades 3 and 7" (University of Oregon Center on Teaching and Learning, 2015).

According to Nagy and Anderson (1984), "an average student in grades 3 through 12 is likely to learn approximately 3,000 new vocabulary words each year, assuming he or she reads between 500,000 and a million running words of text a school year." Similarly, Beck, McKeown, and Kucan (2002) suggest that a student's vocabulary should increase by 2,000–3,000 words a year.

It is recommended by many states and school districts that about 10 percent of these 3,000 words should be taught systematically, across all subject areas a student takes in a given year. So if 300–350 words maximum would be taught explicitly, and the words were divided by the range of content areas in which students participate at the grade level (e.g., math, science, history, literature) in a given year, then only about 60 words can be taught within one subject area each year. Therefore, it is critical that the vocabulary words for instruction be carefully selected so that they represent the most important body of words for that content area and include not just content-specific terminology, but important words that have broader context as well. Given this scenario, it is clearly demonstrated that explicit vocabulary instruction is limiting and cannot be the only way to teach vocabulary.

Academic Vocabulary

There are many words that teachers use in the educational setting that are different from the words used commonly in everyday communications and situations. In order for students to think academically and be poised for school success, they must be familiar with the words that are considered to be part of this specialized vocabulary.

Ordinarily, standard academic words are composed of multiple syllables and tend to be abstract in nature, rather than concrete. "These words express abstract notions (for example, ideology, capacity, and phenomenon), descriptions (for example, ethnic and compatible), processes (for example, decline and trend) and aspects of academic tasks (for example, define, demonstrate, and contrast)" (National Centre of Literacy and Numeracy for Adults, 2012). There are other academic words that are specifically tied directly to particular subject areas, with specialized words for concepts, procedures, instruments, etc. These words are explicit to the content of the subject area. More information on academic vocabulary words will be presented in a subsequent section of this chapter.

Increasing a student's vocabulary is central to school success and improving student achievement. It needs continual, ongoing, and expansive attention. Acquiring a broad vocabulary is the foundation of literacy development at all grade levels. However, it is critical that students in the early grades work intently to increase their knowledge of words. Similarly, it is paramount that students who enter school lagging behind their peers with regard to vocabulary development be afforded customized learning opportunities to jump-start their vocabulary acquisition and use to enable them to move forward in the reading process successfully. The close reading processes with connections to text-dependent questions and citing evidence from the text provide students who need support in building vocabulary with concrete methods for acquiring new words, interacting with them in multiple encounters, and understanding the words' meanings in context. The strategies of close reading have the potential to define a new impetus for students who have traditionally lagged behind.

Connecting Vocabulary with Reading Comprehension

Research has confirmed the irrefutable connection between vocabulary knowledge and reading comprehension (National Reading Technical Assistance Center, 2010). Their report, *A Review of the Current Research on Vocabulary Instruction,* indicates "convergence on the following research themes: (a) frequency of exposure to targeted vocabulary augments children's understanding of word meanings and their use of targeted words, (b) explicit instruction increases word learning, and (c) language engagement through dialogue and/or questioning strategies during a read-aloud enhances word knowledge" (p. 3).

According to Sedita (2005), "One of the oldest findings in educational research is the strong relationship between vocabulary knowledge and reading comprehension. Word knowledge is crucial to reading comprehension and determines how well students will be able to comprehend the texts they read in middle and high school. Comprehension is far more than recognizing words and remembering their meanings. However, if a student does not know the meanings of a sufficient proportion of the words in the text, comprehension is impossible" (p. 1).

Vocabulary knowledge is also "significantly related to decoding, spelling, and school achievement" (Carlisle, 2002, p. 26). The development of vocabulary is a fundamental component of learning, especially in acquiring content knowledge. As students learn, they deepen and expand their academic vocabulary to encompass the growing body of content across subject areas.

The impact of students acquiring a rich and varied vocabulary is significant and its importance to comprehension has been confirmed in recent years (National Institute of Child Health and Human Development (NICHD), 2000). Similarly, Adams (2009) states, "Words are more than words. They are the nexus—the interface—between communication and thought. When we read, it is through words that we build, refine, and modify our knowledge. What makes reading valuable and important are not the words themselves so much as the understandings they afford. The reason we need to know the meanings of words is that they point to the knowledge from which we are to construct, interpret, and reflect on the meaning of the text" (p. 180).

Because students come to school with significantly different levels of word knowledge, teachers in all elementary and middle school grades (three through eight) must continue the work begun in the early grades (preschool through grade two). Teachers must immerse students in classroom settings that are rich in words and word development. Teachers need to provide instruction in and model good oral and written vocabulary knowledge. Daily direct and explicit instruction in word work supports students in the purposeful quest to expand their learning of new and challenging words. Furthermore, teachers need to employ strategies that promote the independent learning of words and incorporate multiple opportunities for students to practice their vocabulary skills and expertise authentically.

The magnitude of students acquiring and developing a robust and wide-ranging vocabulary cannot be emphasized enough. Research supports the widely-held belief that students who possess extensive vocabularies are academically more successful and outperform students whose vocabularies are not as well developed (NICHD, 2000).

Sedita (2005) reports that "vocabulary experts agree that adequate reading comprehension depends on a person already knowing between 90 and 95 percent of the words in a text (Hirsch, 2003). Knowing at least 90 percent of the words enables the reader to get the main idea from the reading and guess correctly what many of the unfamiliar words mean, which will help them learn new words. Readers who do not recognize at least 90 percent of the words will not only have difficulty comprehending the text, but they will miss out on the opportunity to learn new words" (pp. 1–2).

Vocabulary Development and Content-Area Learning

Deepening a student's academic vocabulary scaffolds mastery and achievement, as it is "one of the strongest indicators of how well students will learn subject area content" (Varlas, 2012, p. 1). In English language arts/literacy, this structured approach provides students with a sense of the connections and patterns in language and gives them opportunities to acquire word meanings through reading and listening as well as through writing and speaking.

Logic tells us that students who engage in broad reading become better readers and develop extensive vocabularies. These students are better prepared to interact with content-area readings and content-based assignments. It is also understood that students who are less-than-proficient readers and lag behind their grade-level peers in achievement read less, comprehend less, and know and use fewer words. They would find it complicated and demanding to accomplish assigned reading tasks, including reading content-area requirements and completing content-based assignments.

Vocabulary Instruction and the Common Core

The implementation of Common Core State Standards (CCSS) has pointedly refocused instruction on vocabulary. The CCSS includes three College and Career Readiness (CCR) Anchor Standards for Language (2010) that deal with vocabulary acquisition and use. The CCR standards represent students' summative accomplishment in each area by the end of the K–12 grade spectrum. Even though the standards for vocabulary appear in the language standards, they are fundamental to the context of the reading, writing, and speaking and listening standards. These standards have positioned districts and schools to more prescriptively define curriculum goals and instructional objectives related to accomplishing the proficiency skills expected by the standards at each grade level.

CCSS College and Career Readiness Anchor Standards for Language: Vocabulary Acquisition and Use	
Source: Common Core State Standards (2010)	
CCR 4	Determine or clarify the meaning of unknown and multiple-meaning words and phrases by using context clues, analyzing meaningful word parts, and consulting general and specialized reference materials, as appropriate.
CCR 5	Demonstrate understanding of figurative language, word relationships, and nuances in word meanings.
CCR 6	Acquire and use accurately a range of general academic and domain-specific words and phrases sufficient for reading, writing, speaking, and listening at the college and career readiness level; demonstrate independence in gathering vocabulary knowledge when encountering an unknown term important to comprehension or expression.

The three standards listed above each have grade-level indicators that are expected to be mastered. Here is an overview of the vocabulary skills needing mastery at the eighth-grade level.

CCSS Language Standards: Grade 8
Source: Common Core State Standards (2010)
Vocabulary Acquisition and Use
CCSS.ELA-Literacy.L.8.4: Determine or clarify the meaning of unknown and multiple-meaning words or phrases based on *grade 8 reading and content*, choosing flexibly from a range of strategies. a. Use context (e.g., the overall meaning of a sentence or paragraph; a word's position or function in a sentence) as a clue to the meaning of a word or phrase. b. Use common, grade-appropriate Greek or Latin affixes and roots as clues to the meaning of a word (e.g., *precede, recede, and secede*). c. Consult general and specialized reference materials (e.g., dictionaries, glossaries, thesauruses), both print and digital, to find the pronunciation of a word or determine or clarify its precise meaning or its part of speech. d. Verify the preliminary determination of the meaning of a word or phrase (e.g., by checking the inferred meaning in context or in a dictionary).
CCSS.ELA-Literacy.L.8.5: Demonstrate understanding of figurative language, word relationships, and nuances in word meanings. a. Interpret figures of speech (e.g., verbal irony, puns) in context. b. Use the relationship between particular words to better understand each of the words. c. Distinguish among the connotations (associations) of words with similar denotations (definitions) (e.g., *bullheaded, willful, firm, persistent, resolute*).
CCSS.ELA-Literacy.L.8.6: Acquire and use accurately grade-appropriate general academic and domain-specific words and phrases; gather vocabulary knowledge when considering a word or phrase important to comprehension or expression.

There is one additional expansion of the acquisition of vocabulary associated with the Common Core State Standards. The standards categorize academic vocabulary—the vocabulary students need to develop and be proficient with at their grade level and in the associated content areas—into different levels containing different kinds of words. The categorization for words that are encountered by students in texts is in tiers based on the framework developed and published by Beck, McKeown, and Kucan (2002, 2008), as indicated in the Common Core (Appendix A, 2010). Their framework includes three tiers, or levels, of words in terms of the words' commonality (more or less frequently occurring) and applicability (broader to narrower). Tier One words are everyday words that most students learn in the early grades developmentally and straightforwardly.

Tier Two and Tier Three Academic Vocabulary

TIER TWO ACADEMIC VOCABULARY ("general academic words")	TIER THREE ACADEMIC VOCABULARY ("domain-specific words")
Characteristics and Samples of Words	
Primarily appear in print in all types of written texts Informational texts (*relative, vary, formulate, specificity, accumulate*) Technical texts (*calibrate, itemize, periphery*) Literary texts (*misfortune, dignified, faltered, unabashedly*)	Not frequently used except in specific content areas, domains, or fields of study (*lava, carburetor, legislature, circumference, aorta*)
Represent subtle or more precise forms of familiar works (*saunter* instead of *walk*)	Most important to developing knowledge and building understanding a new concept within a text
Multiple-meaning words (*dread, either, crane, column, tackle, terrific, like, marker, patient, novel*)	More common in informational texts than in literature because of their specificity and close ties to content knowledge
Often used by more experienced users	Recognized as new and "hard" words for most readers (particularly student readers)
Found across many genres and domains	Often explicitly defined by the author of a text, repeatedly used, and otherwise heavily scaffolded (e.g., made a part of a glossary)
Highly generalizable (*fortunate, obvious, ridiculous, complex, establish, verify*)	Medical, legal, scientific (biology, physics), historical, and mathematical terms are all examples of these words (e.g., *algorithm, arbitration, corpuscle, nomadic, nucleus, protons*)
Source: Common Core State Standards, Appendix A, 2010 (p. 33)	

Tier Two words transcend disciplines and are integrated into many content-area subjects. The chart above refers to them as "general academic words." Since the words proliferate many different units of study, Tier Two words should be reinforced in multiple subjects as they are encountered in varied complex text. Additionally, Tier Two words are broader and their definitions cannot be easily detected through clues in the context of the content. In many cases, there is subtlety to the meaning and nuances related to the text type. Tier Two words need to be explicitly taught to students as they are commonly found in complex grade-level texts—both fiction and informational/nonfiction. Tier Two words are important because of their wide use in varied types of reading materials. These words are powerful to students as they develop and increase their vocabulary proficiency and therefore are critical as a body of words that students need to master.

Tier Two words often cause more problems than Tier Three words. The easily explainable reason for this is that Tier Three words, given their uniqueness and content specificity, are usually "introduced by the teacher, often explicitly defined in the text including a glossary, and repeated a number of times in each chapter" (Liben, 2010, p. 2). These supports are not as clear for Tier Two words, given the nature of the words themselves, and are usually not provided by the teacher.

Effective Vocabulary Instruction

An exemplary classroom, when thinking about vocabulary instruction, would be one in which the students are totally involved in a language-rich environment. Both the teacher and the students pay attention to language in its entirety—in all forms, all contexts, etc. In this classroom, there would be evidence to showcase that the entire class (students and teacher) celebrate a love of words when reading, writing, and speaking, and the emphasis on vocabulary would permeate across content areas.

According to the Texas Reading Initiative (2002), "to be effective, a program of vocabulary instruction should provide students with opportunities for word learning by:

- encouraging wide reading
- exposing students to high-quality oral language
- promoting word consciousness
- providing explicit instruction of specific words
- providing modeling and instruction in independent word-learning strategies (p. 11)

Classrooms that exude a language-rich learning environment focus on developing a love of all types of words. Words that are quirky, attention-grabbing, out-of-the-ordinary, and fun will spark students to use them creatively and often. Words that convey feelings and emotions will provide students with new ways to express their passions and their indifference. Words that are difficult, controversial, and/or sophisticated will spur maturity and refinement. Continuous reading opportunities will encourage students to learn new words and grow their vocabularies.

Alignment with Grade-Level Texts

Vocabulary achievement connects directly with the texts students read. The texts need to steadily intensify in complexity over time, both at a grade level and throughout the grades. This means that students need to be reading texts that are considered appropriate for the grade level. This rigor should be aligned with the three-part text complexity model from Chapter 1. (See page 21.) For example, a fifth grader might expand his or her vocabulary *somewhat* from a second- to third-grade text, but far more growth would take place if the student was reading texts written at a fifth-grade or higher level of complexity.

This concept needs to be given thoughtful consideration by teachers as they are considering and selecting texts to be used in lessons and units of study. Even if students are not reading at grade level, they can certainly be exposed to complex, grade-level informational text, provided that the teacher scaffolds the use of the text strategically and supports the text complexity. Compensating for the students' lack of background skills through reading the text aloud, doing close readings for different purposes, and engaging the students in scaffolded skill development in a positive, supported, and structured manner will assist students in persevering through the challenging text. The teacher assists them with gaining knowledge of subject-area content and builds up their learning. In this way, students are not negatively impacted by the possible difficulty of the text itself.

As we have discussed at length in this chapter, there are really two major realms of importance that come to the forefront when planning effective vocabulary instruction: (1) the selection of words to teach and (2) the instructional practices employed to help students learn. So let's take a look at the instruction component now.

Academic Vocabulary Instruction Methods

The National Reading Panel's (NICHD, 2000) "findings on vocabulary yielded several specific implications for teaching reading. First, vocabulary should be taught both directly and indirectly. Repetition and multiple exposures to vocabulary items are important. Learning in rich contexts, incidental learning, and use of computer technology all enhance the acquisition of vocabulary. Direct instruction should include task restructuring as necessary and should actively engage the student. Finally, dependence on a single vocabulary instruction method will not result in optimal learning."

The following gives more details to describe the objectives above.

Direct, Explicit Instruction

Effective vocabulary instruction is exemplified by purposeful word selection. Direct instruction includes teaching specific words (e.g., prereading vocabulary prior to a reading selection) and analyzing word roots, affixes, prefixes, and suffixes.

Indirect, Implicit Instruction

This component focuses on the words to be taught and providing students with ongoing and recurring opportunities for multiple, varied interactions with words in meaningful contexts. Interacting with words in many different ways and in varied contexts results in the robust and enduring learning of words.

By having students read often and read a lot, indirect instruction sets the stage for students to experience many new words. This exposure for students often causes them to have an enlightening interface with word study. It also helps them develop an appreciation for words and experience enjoyment and satisfaction in their use. According to Sedita (2005), indirect instruction teaches all the words students need to learn that one cannot simply teach.

In both instances—direct instruction and indirect instruction—a great deal of emphasis is placed on students to practice to build capacity for learning so that reading fluency and automaticity develop over time and students' reading comprehension, along with learning, increases.

Multimedia Connections

Vocabulary instruction can also be taught utilizing 21st-century concepts of text, such as by using online resources that include graphic representations and hypertext. There are a number of reputable sources for engaging students with online connections to increase their practice and supplement the direct and indirect approaches to learning.

As an extension of the method of instruction described, practice is always emphasized to increase capacity through making reading automatic. Learners are always encouraged to draw connections between what they do know and words they encounter that they do not know.

Conventions of Standard English and Knowledge of Language

This chapter has focused extensively on vocabulary thus far. Vocabulary is one of the two component areas of the Common Core State Standards for language. Vocabulary has natural connections to the prior chapters on reading concepts. There will also be connections with vocabulary made in the next chapter on quality writing. The second component area of the CCSS language standards deals with the conventions of standard English and knowledge of language. See the chart on the next page.

Throughout these three chapters, much has been said about students being able to read fluently and proficiently. By focusing on these standards here, we see how they are interwoven into all of the work that reading instruction implies. As students read various genres, their attention will be drawn to how the author uses standard English, how the text passage is written in grammatically correct fashion, etc.

The standards for conventions of standard English and knowledge of language permeate all the instructional modalities of a comprehensive literacy curriculum. These standards are important and should be treated equally during instructional planning, lesson delivery, and assessment. That is why they are included here.

However, for the purpose of this book, the summative ELA assessments are the focus of our preparation. Presently, on the assessments, there are no discrete tasks that are solely focused on the conventions of standard English. On past state assessments, there might have been tasks requiring students to "revise and edit" writing passages, in which the scoring of those items was directly based on the grammatical skills of revising and editing.

That is not the case on the summative ELA assessments being administered. The assessments do not focus on the discrete skill level, but rather on the implicit learning and mastery through application—in reading, writing, and speaking and listening. These language skills are embedded in every aspect as an underlying foundational element and viewed in the context of the overall impact and importance.

The demonstration of students' knowledge and fluency of the CCSS language standards will be through the extended written responses they construct on the performance assessments as well as their understanding as they read passages and listen to the media clips presented on the tests.

Ultimately, students' mastery of the CCSS language standards coalesces with their mastery of the reading, writing, and speaking and listening standards, with the goal of being prepared for college and careers that demand proficiency at a high level in order to compete globally in the connected world.

CCSS College and Career Readiness Anchor Standards for Language	
Source: Common Core State Standards (2010)	
Conventions of Standard English	
CCR 1	Demonstrate command of the conventions of standard English grammar and usage when writing or speaking.
CCR 2	Demonstrate command of the conventions of standard English capitalization, punctuation, and spelling when writing.
Knowledge of Language	
CCR 3	Apply knowledge of language to understand how language functions in different contexts, to make effective choices for meaning or style, and to comprehend more fully when reading or listening.

CCSS Language Standards: Grade 8

Source: Common Core State Standards (2010)

Conventions of Standard English

CCSS.ELA-Literacy.L.8.1: Demonstrate command of the conventions of standard English grammar and usage when writing or speaking.

a. Explain the function of verbals (gerunds, participles, infinitives) in general and their function in particular sentences.

b. Form and use verbs in the active and passive voice.

c. Form and use verbs in the indicative, imperative, interrogative, conditional, and subjunctive mood.

d. Recognize and correct inappropriate shifts in verb voice and mood.

CCSS.ELA-Literacy.L.8.2: Demonstrate command of the conventions of standard English capitalization, punctuation, and spelling when writing.

a. Use punctuation (comma, ellipsis, dash) to indicate a pause or break.

b. Use an ellipsis to indicate an omission.

c. Spell correctly.

Knowledge of Language

CCSS.ELA-Literacy.L.8.3: Use knowledge of language and its conventions when writing, speaking, reading, or listening.

a. Use verbs in the active and passive voice and in the conditional and subjunctive mood to achieve particular effects (e.g., emphasizing the actor or the action; expressing uncertainty or describing a state contrary to fact).

The inclusion of language standards demonstrates that they are prerequisite skills for college and career readiness. Students must thoroughly understand and exhibit proficiency with English grammar, usage, and mechanics and be able to use language so that it communicates meaning efficiently and successfully. These skills need to be mastered so that students can use language deliberately and correctly throughout their school career and in their lives.

By design, the authors of the CCSS intentionally commingled vocabulary with the language standards. It is the goal that student "be able to determine or clarify the meaning of grade-appropriate words encountered through listening, reading, and media use; come to appreciate that words have nonliteral meanings, shadings of meaning, and relationships to other words; and expand their vocabulary in the course of studying content" (CCSS, p. 25). The fact that the language standards represent an independent strand should not reflect their isolation in use or learning. The language skills acquired through the CCSS indicators are inextricably entwined with the vocabulary expectations as well as reading, writing, and speaking and listening skills required by the standards. The corpus of the standards coalesce as a complete entity and are indivisible.

The Classroom: 10 Practical Strategies on Building Students' Vocabulary Success

1. Create a school-wide culture for language: Develop a vocabulary instructional plan. "A school-wide or district-wide commitment to research-based vocabulary instruction can ensure that there are consistent practices in all classrooms and that there is a cumulative effect on the development of students' vocabulary across subjects and over the years" (Studies & Research Committee of the Massachusetts Reading Association, 2011, p. 2).

It behooves teachers to believe in their school as a professional learning community that is proactive and forward thinking. Developing and instituting a comprehensive and consistent vocabulary curriculum and implementation plan so that all students can be more successful as they move up the grades would be a key grade- and building-level initiative in support of student achievement. Since this plan would spiral with the students as they move forward to each subsequent grade, they can and will build confidence, familiarity, and knowledge in the expected instructional practices associated with the vocabulary instructional plan. This thorough plan will assist students in concentrating their energy on learning new words and ballooning their vocabulary development and usage as their educational career progresses.

2. Increase in-class and home-based independent reading time. Students should be persuaded and supported to read often and in varying contexts as vocabulary is exponentially increased through interacting with texts on a daily basis. The amount of time spent reading and the amount read are both important to students who are developing reading proficiency. An example provided by the Florida Department of Education (2011) highlights that "a student who reads 21 minutes per day outside of school reads almost 2 million words per year. A student who reads less than a minute per day outside of school reads only 8,000 to 21,000 words per year" (p. 1).

Students should have access to a variety of "just-right" reading materials to facilitate the enjoyment of reading. There should also be a spectrum of leveled materials that will support students as they continually progress to becoming better readers.

The variety of materials should include both literary and informational text selections, short and extended texts, myths, fables, plays, song lyrics, news articles, pamphlets, brochures, novels, chapter books, poems, informational manuals, textbooks, reference materials, magazines, newsletters, etc. When a teacher looks at independent reading time through the lens of academic vocabulary improvement and enhancement, students will concentrate on the new words in the texts that they are perusing and will develop contextual ways to learn those new words when they appear in the text for the first time. For example, students who are not familiar with new words will commit the word and its meaning to memory through multiple exposures in the text. They may also use the word correctly in authentic, daily communication with others to ensure comprehension.

3. Select the right vocabulary words for instruction. In making planning decisions about which words to choose for direct instruction, "teachers should focus on words that are important to the text, useful to know in many situations, and that are uncommon in everyday language but recurrent in books" (Juel and Deffes, 2004). Begin by determining the common academic vocabulary words, or the Tier Two words, including content-area words (Tier Three words), that students will come across most frequently or that will be most essential to their learning in a given period of time (e.g., marking period, unit of study, semester, academic year). Choose words that are relevant and apply across content areas and that represent significant, central concepts. Construct a plan based on the words selected.

Selecting the right words also parallels the differentiation of instruction for students. In cases where students in the same class are working on differentiated units of study or texts, the vocabulary selections must match the text in which the students are engaged. It would not be instructionally fruitful to have differentiated small groups for reading, yet work on vocabulary as a whole-class activity. It would be much more beneficial to match the vocabulary words with the work each differentiated group is doing.

According to Beck, McKeown, and Kucan (2002), here are three criteria for teachers to think about as they identify possible words:

- How generally useful is the word? Is it a word that students are likely to encounter in other texts? Will it be of use to students in describing their own experiences?

- How does the word relate to other words, to ideas that students know or have been learning? Does it directly relate to some topic of study in the classroom? Or might it add a dimension to ideas that have been developed?

- What does the word bring to a text or situation? What role does the word play in communicating the meaning of the context in which it is used? What role do the words play in relation to the mood and plot of the story? (pp. 26, 29)

Following these planned strategy steps provides teachers with a clear understanding of how to operationalize vocabulary word selection and, at the same time, create opportunities to form connections among concepts, content, and skills between and among units of study or subject areas.

4. Work on word structures and usage. Learning academic vocabulary requires support for students to become independent learners. Instruction that includes practice and review activities requiring students to think deeply about a word and helping them develop strategies for learning words that can be applied in any context is most effective.

Vocabulary instruction that includes these aspects of words and language usage (Massachusetts Reading Association, 2011, p. 4) provides a solid foundation for students to become independent learners:

- word families
- affixes (prefixes, suffixes), derivational affixes (affix changes part of speech, e.g., *joy—joyful*), inflectional affixes (–*s* noun = plural, –*'s* noun = possessive, –*s* verb = present-tense, third-person singular, –*ing* verb = present participle/gerund, –*ed* verb = simple past tense, –*en* verb = past perfect participle, –*er* = adjective, comparative, –*est* = adjective superlative)
- synonyms and antonyms
- cognates (words that have similar origins), including Greek and Latin roots
- multiple meanings
- idioms and figurative speech

5. Create student vocabulary encounter logs. Students need to know and use vocabulary fluently and deeply, so that over time their cumulative vocabulary knowledge percolates into more complex understanding and has application in multiple contexts. To this end, it can be, according to Sedita (2005), "helpful for students to understand how they gradually learn words. Teachers should encourage students to actively construct links between new information and previously known information about a word" (p. 4). Students who become active in this process and are mindfully aware of the connections will achieve better internalization and recollection of new words.

Dale and O'Rourke (1986) delineated four levels of word knowledge as four statements.

1. I never saw it before.
2. I've heard of it, but I don't know what it means.
3. I recognize it in context—it has something to do with...
4. I know it.

Stahl (2003) tells us that "as we encounter a word repeatedly, more and more information accumulates about that word until we have a vague notion of what it 'means.' As we get more information, we are able to define that word. In fact, McKeown, Beck, Omanson, and Pople (1985) found that while four encounters with a word did not reliably improve reading comprehension, 12 encounters did" (p. 18).

The synthesis of this information can be used to create a simple, student-friendly "Vocabulary Encounter Log" that engages students in collecting evidence of their own learning of new words. The log is envisioned to be in a binder so that pages may be added and moved easily as new words are entered. This format could also be recreated in an online format and maintained online by the student.

The student will record one vocabulary word on each page and complete the entries under each column. Each time a student encounters a new word, he or she will complete another page and complete the entries.

When students encounter the same word again and again in different texts, books, online, etc., they only add the entries to the page already created. The log should expand on a daily basis as students encounter new words in all subject areas. Students will continually add new vocabulary words as they read new texts.

Individualized conferencing will provide teachers with an up-to-date status of students' self-assessment. Partnering students in the learning journey increases their commitment to do better and provides them with specifics of what they need to do to improve. The words students list on in their log also become the basis of their "vocabulary study/use plan" so that they can begin to use the words that they know in everyday conversations, writings, etc. in order to practice using the words correctly.

Name:			
My Vocabulary Encounter Log			
Vocabulary Word		**Write the word here:**	
Date I met the word...	**I read the word in...**	**Here is the sentence...**	**I think it means...**

This formative assessment strategy will give teachers real-time data that can be used to modify and inform future instructional goals and practices. Having students maintain their own log can be a way for them to become more aware of the new words they encounter.

6. Create vocabulary visualizations. To help students represent existing and new vocabulary words, teachers can have them create visual representations of the word's meaning as it is used in the context of the text. These could include the creation of original drawings, symbolic pictures, representations of mental images, kinesthetic movements, etc. Students can use the context of the text to determine a word's meaning. They can also provide a model, definition, or synonym for the word. The goal is for students to use the word frequently throughout the school day and embed it within other instructional activities over time.

Another strategy that can be implemented is using technology-based word-mapping tools. These tools create options for visual representations that are an original and unique configuration generated by the manipulation of text provided by the user. The prominence of specific words in the visual representation is based on the frequency of the word in the text. In using these tools, students learn to develop visual displays that highlight the relationships between words in the text they are using.

These three online word-mapping tools are student friendly and effective for the purposes of our discussion. Teachers can use these suggested sites in many different ways that dovetail with their lesson plans.

- VocabGrabber—Analyzes any text and generates a list of the most useful vocabulary words; shows how those words are used in context.
- Wordle—Generates "word clouds" from text provided by the user. The clouds give greater prominence to words that appear more frequently in the source text. This is a free tool and can be used anonymously. The shape of the word cloud can be manipulated to align with the message of the text.
- Wordsift—Sifts through a text passage that is cut and pasted to identify important words that appear in the text. The site creates a word capture, with frequent words being tagged and featured. The word visualization that is created can become the source of rich discussion in classroom settings.

These word-mapping tools can be utilized by teachers in:
- lesson planning preparation
- previewing text
- class and group activities
- learning center stations
- literacy support
- assessment

7. Have fun learning with online vocabulary games. Sometimes students just have to have fun! Learning new vocabulary words can be enjoyable. Students can engage in learning activities to enrich their vocabulary while interacting with online games. Playing word and vocabulary games motivates them. There are many traditional vocabulary games that are very effective. Students of all ages enjoy playing concentration with vocabulary words; using flashcards and matching definitions; and completing anagrams, word searches, and crossword puzzles. There are also several commercially available and online word games kids love.

Just a note of advice. There are thousands of vocabulary word-game sites online. Many of them have .com Internet addresses. Sometimes these are filled with ads that are not student-friendly. There are plenty of .com sites that are reputable and educational in nature, offer a variety of activities that focus on words and word meanings, and are free. A list at the end of this chapter identifies sites that feature vocabulary-focused games, which provide much enjoyment and a great deal of learning.

8. Assemble a rockin' classroom library. Books, books, and more books! The primary way in which students can acquire an abundance of words, or word wealth, is for them to read books. All different kinds of books. Books about a variety of subjects and topics. Classroom libraries provide the most convenient opportunities for students to access an array of reading materials that capitalize on the connections to subject-area topics and their personal interests and also encourage exploration of unknown topics, stories, historical accounts, etc. Classroom teachers are adept at amassing and growing an ever-increasing collection of pertinent books that are topically related to areas under study.

Having students read multiple texts on the same subject helps sequence their knowledge into deeper explorations. Similarly, having students read popular or trade books on a particular topic or type of information helps to increase their background knowledge and bridge them into more difficult textbook readings, etc. Textbook publishers sometimes provide complimentary copies of fiction and nonfiction books on topics related to areas of study in science, social studies, literature, and the arts.

It is important that the classroom library resources continually expand and include new offerings. If this project works effectively, certainly books will disappear as students take them home for independent reading. (And isn't that the goal—to have students develop a passion for books?) So a steady stream of new books needs to appear. Secondly, as the knowledge levels and reading levels escalate throughout the year, more challenging levels of books will need to be infused into the collection to meet the spiraling of student growth.

9. Activate vocabulary learning through the performing arts: drama, dance, and music. Drama and dance are forms of communication in which the performer conveys meaning through interpretation and a presentation. Movement, dance, and drama are powerful modes that teachers can use to complement vocabulary acquisition and reinforce learning.

Acting assists students in developing literacy skills. Drama and movement stimulate the brain to learn. In turn, brain-based learning facilitates the retention of information.

According to Giovanoni, Hanaoka, and Pascarella (2010), acting is an effective strategy for teachers to employ in literacy development because it provides notable benefits:

- promotes increased motivation and reduced anxiety;
- is a highly motivating approach for students to process and share information;
- helps with learning new words by associating the meaning with the physical response;
- requires listening, which is a key to language development; and
- enhances creative thinking, social interaction, and problem-solving.

There is a body of evidence that has proven dance can improve literacy. For some students, visual and auditory learning is not their primary style of learning. For students who are kinesthetic learners, incorporating movement into their learning can significantly influence their quality of learning and their learning outcomes. Dancing out a series of vocabulary words to form a sentence or a poem can solidify meaning and themes for students.

Exploring words through improvisation is another way for students to get involved with vocabulary development. Dancing out the meaning of a word or words in the text can create a relationship to the text, which may have proved elusive before.

Teachers can also encourage students to sing out their vocabulary words. Music connects to a different part of the brain than oral language. The singing of syllables and word parts, rhyming words, and new vocabulary words may assist some students in better understanding the sound of the word and the patterns.

These kinesthetic connections and the use of various intelligences can make concrete vocabulary learning for students. It is certainly worth the attempt to try new methods. In many cases, students think that learning this way is "not really learning" but fun and enjoyable.

10. Create "Vocabulary Alive!" journals. Vocabulary-minded students are aware of the words around them (in conversations, in reading materials, and in school textbooks) and enjoy learning new words. One approach for vocabulary to become alive for students is by promoting sophisticated words. For example, replace common, everyday words with higher-level, unfamiliar words that have the same meaning (e.g., "eat" vs. "scarf" or "consume"). This refinement creates word acuity. In developing this keen awareness of vocabulary, students will be exposed to the use of idiomatic expressions, unique verbal images, vivid descriptions, figurative language (e.g., attention-grabbing metaphors, similes), and plays on words. Dialogue should occur in which the words are pointed out by teachers and discussed with students. Teachers should provide opportunities that develop students' interest in words, delve into the subtle meanings of words, seize upon how to have fun with words, and clarify how words and concepts are related across different contexts.

Since the goal is for vocabulary—both personal and academic—to flourish in a lively way, students can be asked to create a personal "Vocabulary Alive!" journal. Upon encountering new and unique words, exciting phrases, and creatively expressed thoughts in their reading, students should select examples and record them in their journals. These examples of rich, stimulating vocabulary should be shared with other students, placed on a word-of-the-day chart, etc.

The "Vocabulary Alive!" journal is expected to be embedded in classroom daily practice as an ongoing guided and independent learning activity for all students. Students self-select words and terms to be studied. These words can be chosen from class texts, units of study, extended texts, etc., and students write them in their journals. A format for students to record their word involves a three-step process:

- Write down the word in the sentence from the original source.
- Guesstimate the word meaning from the context and add it to the entry.
- Write the dictionary definition.

Students are then directed to complete three active-learning research tasks:

- Locate the word in an authentic, real-life situation (newspaper, the Internet, trade book, television, textbook, podcast, webinar, etc.).
- Record the real-life sentence in his/her journal entry and think about how the entry connects to what the student wrote initially.
- After analyzing all of the pieces of evidence he/she has about the word, write something to make a core connection with the word. The student could revise his/her writing, add a more explanatory definition, give examples of what the word means, or make some other meaningful connection. Students might extend this section by including pictures representing their word.

The "Vocabulary Alive!" journal is meant to be an enjoyable activity for students. Keeping the journal should not be a chore but a learning experience that becomes part of the student's practice through the grades.

Online Resources for Extending Learning

These online websites provide vocabulary games, activities, strategies, and much more for teachers to use for word work with students.

- Dictionary.com—Dictionary and thesaurus with definitions, synonyms, antonyms, idioms, word origins, quotes, audio pronunciations, and example sentences.

- PBS Kids Games and Vocabulary—Numerous games focused on vocabulary words and tips. Colorful animations look like video games when played.

- The Teacher's Corner—Generates a completely free crossword puzzle with your vocabulary words. Choose fonts, images, and colors. Also creates word search puzzles.

- Visual Thesaurus/ThinkMap—The Visual Thesaurus is a 3-D interactive reference tool, powered by ThinkMap, that gets students of all ages excited about words. Using visualization technology, the Visual Thesaurus takes a unique and remarkably beautiful approach to presenting the results of a word that has been looked up. It creates an animated display of words and meanings—a visual representation of the English language. The ThinkMap visualization places a word in the center of the display, connected to related words and meanings.

- Vocabulary.com—Provides challenges to improve vocabulary through an adaptive learning system, combined with the world's fastest dictionary, so that words can be learned more quickly and more efficiently. The site uses the most essential English vocabulary words, words needed in academic settings, and words from books, periodicals, and other material to cumulatively amass more than 1.6 billion words. The site provides analysis of achievements and reinforces skills by reintroducing words at various times to make sure they are being retained.

- Vocabulary Can Be Fun!—Flash online word games including online word searches and crossword puzzles. Users choose the vocabulary list that the online word game will utilize. The vocabulary games are popular for use on interactive whiteboards to build vocabulary skills in classrooms.

- World Wide Words—Offers a word of the day, free word searches, and word meanings along with access to online dictionaries.

- Word Buff—Shares expert tips, game strategies, and vocabulary learning and memory techniques for people who play word games. The advice comes from the world's best wordsmiths and memory game experts. There are many interesting and unique vocabulary games that have been contributed to this site (e.g., "Pass the Dictionary").

Summary

Chapter 3 provides compelling information on how vocabulary contributes to reading comprehension and enhances the development of the spectrum of reading skills. Vocabulary work should be an integral component of every teacher's lessons, in all grade levels, and across all subject areas.

Beginning in the early grades, working with words provides growth, kernel by kernel, as students learn new words. Each kernel is an essential part of the core learning that enriches students' conversational ability as well as contributes to their specialized language engagement in the academic setting. As students progress through the grades, vocabulary enrichment expands and continues to be a critical skill, given the research that shows students' vocabularies double between grades three and seven. Teachers at these grade levels can monopolize students' time and energy by engaging them in learning and using new words through fun and exciting games.

The Tier Two and Tier Three words that students encounter multiple times in multiple situations at each grade level are important words that layer like protective armor as students learn and apply them. This academic vocabulary development is integral to successfully shifting the paradigm from "learning to read" to "reading to learn." When students enter middle and high school, the volume of new vocabulary explodes as experiential student learning multiplies.

If our goal is to prepare students for college and their future careers, students must be able to use vocabulary to communicate deliberately and effectively—negotiating, conversing, discussing, bargaining, conferring, and consulting. As we will see in the next chapter, vocabulary expertise is definitively a significant and essential skill in writing competence.

CHAPTER 4:
Maximizing Quality Writing: Opinion/ Argument, Informational/Explanatory, and Narrative

In the first three chapters of this book, the focus was on the importance of students being proficient readers. Close reading emphasizes the skills vital for thinking about and analyzing what they've read. This chapter connects reading with quality writing so that writing is positioned equally and importantly. Writing is an essential skill that is elemental to engaging in all types of activities: professional, social, community, and civic. Students need to write clearly and effectively about what they've read, what they've learned, and what they think in order to be successful in school, at home, and as community members. Students also need to write creatively and expressively to author original stories, essays, novels, dramas, poetry, and songs.

There is no aspect of the days of our busy, global-based lives that do not represent written content in some manner. Books, movies, advertising, magazines, political campaigns, newspapers, theatrical productions, musical recordings, financial documents, medical records, instructional manuals, and website content are all developed from written content that materializes in different formulations, creating something inventive, original, resourceful, or important.

In *Writing Next: Effective Strategies to Improve Writing of Adolescents in Middle and High Schools—A Report to Carnegie Corporation of New York* (Graham and Perin, 2007), Vartan Gregorian, president of the Carnegie Corporation, tells us that "indeed, young people who do not have the ability to transform thoughts, experiences, and ideas into written words are in danger of losing touch with the joy of inquiry, the sense of intellectual curiosity, and the inestimable satisfaction of acquiring wisdom that are the touchstones of humanity" (p. 1).

Writing helps us transform our thoughts into words. Writing involves the skill of scribing coherent words on paper and composing text. Producing connected text (sentences, paragraphs, and documents) communicates ideas or information. Writing goes beyond the rudiments of grammar. Writing is a true manifestation of learning.

This chapter opens with a solid rationale for recognizing that all students must achieve writing proficiency if they are going to become high-achieving students and highly successful adults. There are critical, life-changing elements that elucidate why writing is a fundamental skill in which today's students must achieve a high level of proficiency. The chapter next provides an overview of the broad work that the summative ELA assessments aligned to national and/or state standards will encompass.

The chapter explores the elements of quality writing instruction through the writing process, the value of conferencing with student writers, and the reasons why writing is the essence of effective communication. It looks at how opinion and argument-based writing, informational and explanatory writing, and even narrative writing, can powerfully change the communication landscape, depending on the purpose and the audience. There is great depth in the information provided on the Common Core State Standards and the focus on writing instruction. Through the College and Career Readiness Anchor Standards for Writing, we get to see a very clear vision for mastery of skills in a progression through the school years and how this concentration of effort, skill development, and writing craft interplays with reading achievement, vocabulary development, and speaking and listening.

The chapter concludes with practical guidance. The presentation of 10 effective classroom strategies for teachers to consider can further their commitment to making writing a priority in their classrooms.

Why Is Writing Important?

"If students are to make knowledge their own, they must struggle with the details, wrestle with the facts, and rework raw information and dimly understood concepts into language they can communicate to someone else. In short, if students care to learn, they must write" (National Commission on Writing in America's Schools and Colleges, 2003, p. 9).

Educators have the responsibility of ensuring that students learn to write and write well so that they may carry out their lives from today forward as youngsters and as future adults, in school, at home, and in society. As we prepare today's students for their future careers and their role as citizens, present-day school experiences must provide students with writing instruction that produces adept, confident writers.

Strong writers convey their ideas competently, efficiently, and powerfully. It is critical that students be able to produce quality written work and communicate in writing for a range of purposes and to a variety of audiences. Major American corporations indicate that writing is a "threshold skill" for hiring and promotion among salaried, professional employees (College Entrance Examination Board, 2004, p. 3).

All educators are charged with this goal—that students will be well equipped as writers when they enter college and make career choices. In 2012, of the 3.2 million high school graduates, some 2.1 million, or 66 percent, enrolled in college the following fall (National Center for Education Statistics, 2014). Students are deeply interested in a college degree because it positions them for improved workplace opportunities and career possibilities. Writing competence will only assist in this goal. It helps students accomplish difficult assignments, builds their confidence, deepens their capabilities with analyzing and evaluating written material, and emboldens their creativity and originality in producing written critiques, investigations, and research.

Writing is a developmental process that blossoms through practice and spirals with mastery of skills at each grade level. It helps students understand what they know, because they can process the learning and translate their understanding into coherent words/text on paper. Students need to write more often and more deeply to become more prolific writers. "Writing today is not the frill for the few, but an essential skill for the many" (National Commission on Writing in America's Schools and Colleges, 2003, p. 11).

In *Teaching Elementary School Students to be Effective Writers: A Practice Guide*, education professionals are provided with evidence-based recommendations that address the challenge of teaching writing to young students. The authors of this research-based report inform us that "Writing, like reading...begins with the acquisition of foundational skills and then leads to the application of more sophisticated techniques. For younger students, for example, 'writing' activities could include interpretive drawing, invented spelling, or interactive writing. Although these activities are not often considered traditional writing experiences, they accomplish the same goals: helping students communicate thoughts and ideas to others, encouraging them to engage with the text to deepen their understanding of the content, and drawing connections to prior learning experiences" (Graham, Bollinger, Olson, D'Aoust, MacArthur, McCutchen, and Olinghouse, 2012, p. 6).

It would be natural for narrative writing to be the mode of writing that students focus on in early grades as it corresponds to the developmental nature of language acquisition and vocabulary development as well as connects with the world of the student in and out of school. Students are focused on learning to read and, therefore, to write. For instance, in English language arts/literacy, a good part of reading instruction is focused on fiction texts, and in social studies, students are learning about their neighborhood, their families, and their local community members. Narrative writing is a natural outgrowth to storytelling, fables, fiction, poetry, songs, etc.

As the grade level increases, the focus shifts in classrooms from "learning to read" to "reading to learn," which delves into a content-focused, performance-structured experience for students. A great deal of informational/explanatory text reading occurs in various content areas on historical, scientific, and technical content. Accordingly, shifting the focus to writing arguments or informational pieces that analyze sources (including writing about research students have performed) becomes the norm.

According to Graham and Hebert (2010), "having students write about what they read, whether by taking notes or answering questions about a text, or construct a summary or an extended written response regarding what they have read, students improve both their reading comprehension and their writing skills when writing in response to texts" (p. 5).

Summative Assessments: What to Expect

The goal of the summative ELA assessments aligned with national and/or state standards is to assess if students can write properly and proficiently on substantive topics to meet the demands they will face in all levels of schooling and their career choices. The summative ELA assessments expect students to write with fluency, skill, and independence. Writing effectiveness gives primary importance to using and/or analyzing sources.

The passages and source materials will represent information students are learning in the content areas at their grade level. Content in science, social studies (history, geography, and civics), health, and the arts will be the prime sources of the text passages and source materials.

Focus on Writing Purposes

The summative ELA assessments include the performance assessment component. It is on the performance assessment that students will participate in three different writing tasks, one for each writing purpose.

There are three broad rhetorical writing purposes that will make up the tasks: opinion/argument writing, informational/explanatory writing, and narrative writing. Students will write extended responses in the form of essays for each of these three purposes. Each essay must include relevant evidence extracted from the text sources provided, including multimedia sources—with which students will interact as part of the reading/writing connection.

Opinion/Argument

- Students in grades 3–5 will be expected to write an essay, which requires them to form and defend an opinion, supported by information provided in the text passages and source materials.
- Students in grades 6–8 will be expected to compose an argument, using evidence from the text passages and source materials to form and support claims and counterclaims.

Informational/Explanatory

- Students in grades 3–5 will be expected to write an informative essay, report, etc., using facts and data found in the text passages and source materials and synthesizing the facts and data. Students will develop a written response to the writing prompt that will inform an audience about a topic, issue, problem, etc.

- Students in grades 6–8 will be expected to write to the explanatory purpose, analyzing source material to explain some aspect of a subject. Students' written response will clarify, advise, or instruct the reader on some topic, problem, or issue, based on the writing prompt.

Narrative

- Students in grades 3–8 will be expected to write to the narrative purpose, using information in the sources as inspiration to write a story, capture the essence of an experience, or generate a sequel. The narrative response is usually correlated with a fiction selection that is interesting and grade appropriate.

For each writing purpose or category, students will be assigned one grade-level appropriate task. There will be a total of three writing tasks to be completed by the students. They will complete the three writing assignments on the performance assessment. The task types that students may see are described in the next section.

Regardless of the writing form, students are expected to write quality responses that meet these requirements:

- present a well-developed introduction that effectively frames the prompt's issue and writer's argument; present a well-developed conclusion that extends the essay's ideas;

- maintain a focus on discussing the specific issue in the prompt throughout the essay;

- provide development in support of ideas; extend ideas by using specific, logical reasons and illustrative examples;

- provide a unified, coherent organizational structure that presents a logical progression of ideas; and

- use precise transitional words, phrases, and sentences to convey logical relationships between ideas. (Extrapolated from the ACT College and Career Readiness Standards—Writing, 2014, pp. 1–5)

Focus on Writing Tasks

The three writing purposes were described on the prior pages. The reading purposes tie in neatly with the writing tasks. There will be three writing tasks that students will complete:

- a research simulation writing task;
- a literary analysis writing task; and
- a narrative writing task.

As part of the assignment for each writing task, students will read (view or listen to) one or more passages (or multimedia) related to a topic. In grade 3, they will read (view or listen to) two test passages total. For grades 4–8, students will read (view or listen to) three text passages. Next, they will provide responses to several text-based questions to assess comprehension of each text. Correspondingly, students will synthesize information gathered from the source materials, finalize their thoughts, and compose an analytical, extended written response.

Each writing performance task clearly defines the expected writing form or product that students need to produce. These forms include, but are not limited to, writing a letter, constructing a report, preparing a speech (written), and creating an essay. As assessment products in the upper grades represent the rigor of the grade level, sophistication in the student-generated products increases significantly. The assessments value reciprocal connections between reading and writing, which strategically inform students' construction and development of written products.

The three types of writing tasks described will incorporate opinion/argument writing. Students are expected to construct and write an analytical essay based on the prompt or task given on the summative assessment. They are encouraged to provide their thoughts and opinions as a seminal element of the writing product. Their opinions should be supported with factual evidence and statistics so that a strong argument can be produced. For grades 3–5, students are expected to ground their responses as opinion-focused written responses. In grades 6–8, argument based writing is the expected threshold for extended written responses on the summative ELA assessments. This is in keeping with the grade-level writing standards.

Research Simulation Writing Task

Research is a curriculum expectation for each grade level participating in the summative ELA assessments aligned with national and/or state standards. The research performance tasks will be situational, grade appropriate, and based on a critical issue that students are inspired to delve into more deeply. The task will motivate students to learn about a problem, question, circumstance, issue, etc. based on reading source information.

CCR Writing Anchor Standard 7 (Common Core State Standards, 2010) details that at each grade level, students are expected to do research and then present their knowledge. The standard indicates that they should "conduct short as well as more sustained research projects" (CCR 7).

Since students are expected to present their knowledge as a result of having done the research, they will be required to conduct a simulation of a research episode on the summative ELA assessments. Their results will be reported through an extended written response demonstrating their knowledge. The response format will be an analytic and/or informative essay. Students are to showcase their skills of observation, deduction, and proper use and evaluation of evidence across text types.

In most grade levels, students will be poised to interact with three sources of information. It will be a combination of print resources, video clips, and audio clips. The first text passage (or multimedia source) will usually be the anchor text, which introduces students to the topic. Students will read it thoroughly and answer a series of text-based questions to ensure their understanding of the piece. Students will then engage with one or two other text sources that are related to the anchor text. They will answer several questions about each of those texts. Having read all three texts (or a combination with multimedia), students will synthesize their thinking and formalize their notes. Students will then write a formal extended response to the prompt provided. The writing piece will take the form of an analytic essay. The prompt will instruct students what the task entails and to respond with evidence from one or more of the texts.

The testing time period for this session is the most substantial so that students can do a genuine review of the source materials being presented and still maintain sufficient time to write their response. At all grade levels, students are provided approximately 90 minutes to complete the tasks associated with the research simulation.

Literary Analysis Task

Literature continues to hold a prominent place on the summative ELA assessments. Students will be involved in a task that focuses on reading literature passages (or viewing or listening) and writing an extended response to a prompt.

In most cases, students will read two literature-based texts and provide an analysis comparing and contrasting some key aspect related to both pieces. The written product will be in the form of an analytic essay.

Narrative Writing Task

Narrative writing elaborates on a sequence of events, either actual or invented, that occurs over time. Narratives also convey experiences and can be fiction or nonfiction by design. The narrative writing task on the summative ELA assessments take writing to a new level. First, students will read a narrative anchor text and then write a story, describe a version of events or scenes, predict the next chapter, or write an ending to what they have read. Nonfiction narratives can encompass detailing a scientific process, etc.

On the summative ELA assessments, the narrative writing tasks define the form of the products students need to create. These include writing a journal entry, writing a story, and creating a sequel. Narratives may include personal essays, memoirs, fictional stories, biographical sketches (or profiles), and autobiographies, in addition to short stories and plays.

Designated audiences will be identified and based upon the students' grade level, the purpose, and the task situation. In the earlier grades, students may write to specific and familiar audiences. These could include classmates, parents, a coach, or a principal. For older students, the designated audiences would be of a broader, more general type. These could include the board of education, legislative bodies, Internet audiences, etc.

Focus on Scoring Rubrics

Scoring rubrics have been produced for each writing purpose. There are different rubrics for the narrative purpose, the informational/explanatory purpose, and the opinion/argument purpose.

For students to be successful on the writing assessment, they must be able to write independently and showcase their deep understanding of the writing task. Successful students can synthesize the information and use it in a written response. More specifically, they can connect the questions to the text, find text-based information as evidence to the question, and write succinctly using this evidence as rationale toward a claim.

In this chapter, the summative ELA assessments were discussed at length. There are many aspects of the writing tasks that are commingled into one performance assessment session. Students will need to be cognizant of the writing purpose (opinion/argument, informational/explanatory, or narrative). They also need to be concerned with the performance task type—whether it's research based, a literary analysis, or a narrative. Next, students need to assess what the actual writing prompt is asking them to complete. What will answer the question as it relates to the reading of the provided materials the students have been assigned? Lastly, students need to consider the scoring rubric to ensure that their response hits all of the targeted elements in order to obtain a rating reflecting competent performance.

In order to teach students to be competent and confident writers, explicit teaching and implicit learning must occur simultaneously and continuously. One of the proven strategies to make this work is to have a strong, sequential writing program in place so that students have the opportunity to write. Writing is a lifelong process. Students need to understand that it is a practice-based set of skills. Schools may need to revisit their existing writing goals, objectives, and implementation plans. The plan now is to work toward meeting the new standards and focus on the expectations of the summative ELA assessment tasks.

The next section provides educators with information on the writing process as a model of one plan to improve writing.

The Writing Process

Writing effectively is process oriented. Students, as writers, are required to pay attention to the purpose for writing and understand what the reader needs to know. They especially need to plan what to say and how to say it.

Teachers can help students become effective writers by explicitly teaching them strategies for carrying out each component of the writing process. Teachers should also model classroom strategies for writing. The goal is to support students as they apply the strategies until they are able to sustain them independently.

One such strategy is purpose. It is important for students to learn that writing is used for many different purposes, and this notion should be taught through modeled writing and experience-based writing. Writing is used to share an event or experience, convey information, offer an opinion, persuade someone to change his/her view, take a stand (make an argument), reflect on personal thoughts and ideas, and provide better understanding of something that is read.

Writing instruction could also teach students how genres, or specific forms of writing, are defined by specialized features and elements. Knowing how distinct genres may be connected to different writing purposes helps students better understand their assignments. Using various genres as guiding structures helps students think about what they plan to write, rather than how to write it, so that their written response is more effective in its delivery and connection to the reader.

The writing process provides a structure that guides writers though flexible elements to assist them in the creation of text. Students need to understand that the process involves all of the elements, but not as a linear progression as in a checklist or a graphic organizer. Instead, it is recursive.

An overview of the writing process is provided in the following chart.

The Writing Process	
Planning	Planning involves developing ideas and generating ideas; gathering information from reading, prior knowledge, and discussion with others; and organizing ideas for writing based on the purpose for the text. Students should write down these goals and ideas, so they can refer to and modify them throughout the writing process.
Drafting	Drafting focuses on creating a preliminary version of a text. When drafting, students must select the words and construct the sentences that most accurately convey their ideas, and then transcribe those words and sentences into written language. Skills, such as spelling, handwriting, and capitalization and punctuation also are important when drafting, but these skills should not be the focus of students' effort at this stage.
Sharing	Sharing ideas or drafts with teachers, other adults, and peers throughout the writing process enables students to obtain feedback and suggestions for improving their writing.
Evaluating	Evaluating can be carried out by individual writers as they reread all or part of their text and carefully consider whether they are meeting their original writing goals. Evaluation can also be conducted by teachers and peers who provide the writer with feedback.
Revising	Revising and editing require that writers make changes to their text based on evaluations of their writing. Revising involves making content changes after students first have evaluated problems within their text that obscure their intended meaning. Students should make changes to clarify or enhance their meaning. These changes may include reorganizing their ideas, adding or removing whole sections of text, and refining their word choice and sentence structure.
Editing	Editing involves making changes to ensure that a text correctly adheres to the conventions of written English. Students should be particularly concerned with reviewing their spelling and grammar and making any necessary corrections. Editing changes make a text readable for external audiences and can make the writer's intended meaning clearer.
Publishing	Publishing typically occurs at the end of the writing process, as students produce a final product that is shared publicly in written form, oral form, or both. Not all student writing needs to be published, but students should be given opportunities to publish their writing and celebrate their accomplishments.

Graham, S., Bollinger, A., Booth Olson, C., D'Aoust, C. MacArthur, C., McCutchen, D. & Olinghouse, N. (2012). Teaching Elementary School Students to Be Effective Writers: A Practice Guide (NCEE 2012– 4058). Washington, DC: National Center for Education Evaluation and Regional Assistance, Institute of Education Sciences, U.S. Department of Education, 2012, p. 14.

The Value of Conferencing with Student Writers

The writing conference is a one-on-one protocol between the teacher and a student that is central to the writing process. It provides teachers with a rich opportunity for individualizing instruction based on a student's unique needs. Conferencing can occur at any point in the writing process. It should be a conversation focused on the complex processes and skills involved in writing, but it should be masterfully orchestrated so that the student feels he or she is part of the solution, rather than a problematic writer who needs to meet with the teacher because of writing flaws. Individual conferences generally are short—about two to five minutes—and occur while the other students are involved in their own independent writing projects.

Conferencing is important because it can cover a range of writing skills, strategies, and concepts with which the student needs help. The goal is to create independent writers who are self-reflective and ask questions about their own work.

Several questions can elicit responses from students that help teachers assess students' status in the recurring cycle of improving their writing.

- Does what I have written make sense? Is it logical?
- Does what I have written state what I mean? What else do I need or want to say?
- Did I answer the question? Solve the problem? Address the task?
- What questions might the reader ask after reading what I wrote?
- How can I improve it and make it better or more understandable?

Conferencing notes should be taken by the teacher and the student so that future conferences can pick up in quick fashion from the prior conversation, as conferencing time is intended to be brief.

The Vocabulary Connection

Chapter 3 provided an in-depth discussion of the importance of vocabulary in reading and included inferences and connections to writing. Everything that was offered in that chapter applies to writing instruction and writing activities as well.

Just as students need a wide and deep vocabulary they can apply in many different reading situations, they need to be able to draw on a rich and comprehensive vocabulary if they are to convey their thinking to others by writing too.

Writing and the Common Core

The Common Core State Standards present a game changer for educators when it comes to writing instruction. The standards formulate an explicit and coherent plan for intense student writing experiences throughout the grades, beginning in kindergarten, that center student writing on three broad rhetorical purposes: opinion/argument writing, informational/explanatory writing, and narrative writing.

The instructional shifts embedded in the standards catapult students into more frequent and rigorous work in the first two modes listed above. Shifting the engagement balance levels in third grade to 65 percent analytical writing (30 percent opinions and 35 percent to inform/explain) and 35 percent narrative writing tremendously changes the way elementary teachers need to approach writing. The standards are also recommending a mix of on-demand and review/revise writing assignments within those three modes. At the eighth-grade level, the balance shifts a bit more to 70 percent analytical writing (35 percent opinions and 35 percent to inform/explain) and 30 percent narrative writing (Student Achievement Partners, 2013).

Since these standards represent college- and career-focused skills, it is expected that technological-based writing experiences be embedded into the writing instruction process so that students utilize online technologies for the construction and revising/editing process to improve their written products. This technological proficiency is also necessary for success on the newly developed summative ELA assessments aligned to national and/or state standards being administered.

There are only 10 writing standards, and the "top three" standards are designed to rigorously focus on the three types of purposeful writing as the foundational standards for college- and career-readiness preparation. This conjectures that students would be writing to the standards every day, producing numerous pieces over short and extended time frames throughout the year. To meet the established goals, students will need to devote significant time and effort to writing.

Through these different modes of writing, students need to better employ writing as a way of showcasing their skills and abilities throughout their school activities, assignments, and class work. Writing in the content areas in which they are studying also provides students with the vehicle for representing their work with sophistication, insight, and skill.

One of the more subtle aspects of the CCSS is that students will always be learning the skills for becoming proficient readers along with the skills that are necessary for becoming effective writers—simultaneously. These two global educational goals are inextricably commingled, and the skills through the grades are recursive and connected. There is also a groundswell occurring that will integrate reading and writing more concretely across the content areas of history/social studies, science, and technical subjects and emulate the writing practices being proffered in English language arts/literacy classrooms. This transformation will make the links for student expectations and performances more cohesive, infinitely clearer, and noticeably more consistent. This coherence should make the procedural and operational implementation more student-centered.

As students develop necessary skills and become more prolific in their writing, they learn to recognize that a key purpose of writing is to communicate clearly to an external, sometimes unfamiliar audience and they initiate adaptations to the format and content of their writing to accomplish a specific task and purpose.

The following chart spells out the specifications of the 10 College and Career Readiness Anchor Standards for Writing for students. These are the global representations of what students should be able to do by the time they graduate from high school. There are specific grade-level indicators for each of the 10 standards for each grade level K–12. All of the writing standards begin in kindergarten and spiral up with each grade level through grade 12. The planned vision is that students would be engaged intensely, with rigor, on these skills for 13 years with the goal of mastery and proficiency expected.

CCSS College and Career Readiness Anchor Standards for Writing

Source: Common Core State Standards (2010)

Text Types and Purposes

CCR 1	Write arguments to support claims in an analysis of substantive topics or texts, using valid reasoning and relevant and sufficient evidence.
CCR 2	Write informative/explanatory texts to examine and convey complex ideas and information clearly and accurately through the effective selection, organization, and analysis of content.
CCR 3	Write narratives to develop real or imagined experiences or events using effective technique, well-chosen details, and well-structured event sequences.

Production and Distribution of Writing

CCR 4	Produce clear and coherent writing in which the development, organization, and style are appropriate to task, purpose, and audience.
CCR 5	Develop and strengthen writing as needed by planning, revising, editing, rewriting, or trying a new approach.
CCR 6	Use technology, including the Internet, to produce and publish writing and to interact and collaborate with others.

Research to Build and Present Knowledge

CCR 7	Conduct short as well as more sustained research projects based on focused questions, demonstrating understanding of the subject under investigation.
CCR 8	Gather relevant information from multiple print and digital sources, assess the credibility and accuracy of each source, and integrate the information while avoiding plagiarism.
CCR 9	Draw evidence from literary or informational texts to support analysis, reflection, and research.

Range of Writing

CCR 10	Write routinely over extended time frames (time for research, reflection, and revision) and shorter time frames (a single sitting or a day or two) for a range of tasks, purposes, and audiences.

The Common Core (CCSS Appendix A, p. 23) gives us very clear definitions of what is entailed in the three writing purposes—opinion/argument, informational/explanatory, and narrative. This information is insightful for teachers who are providing instruction. As they plan their yearlong curriculum, instruction, and assessment goals, these attributes can be at the forefront of their planning.

I have chosen to highlight the definition for argument below. You can clearly see from the definition that the writing goal in this area has moved far beyond formulaic thinking. It provides a look into how students will have to analyze and evaluate ideas and information and synthesize the thinking into a presentation. The journey to get to the completed product is the process. The final product is, in essence, the embodiment of the work.

> Argument: Arguments are used for many purposes—to change the reader's point of view, to bring about some action on the reader's part, or to ask the reader to accept the writer's explanation or evaluation of a concept, issue, or problem. An argument is a reasoned, logical way of demonstrating that the writer's position, belief, or conclusion is valid.
>
> - In English language arts/literacy, students make claims about the worth or meaning of a literary work or works. They defend their interpretations or judgments with evidence from the text(s) they are writing about.
>
> - In history/social studies, students analyze evidence from multiple primary and secondary sources to advance a claim that is best supported by the evidence, and they argue for an historically or empirically situated interpretation.
>
> - In science, students make claims in the form of statements or conclusions that answer questions or address problems. Using data in a scientifically acceptable form, students marshal evidence and draw on their understanding of scientific concepts to argue in support of their claims.
>
> (CCSS Appendix A, p.23)

There are very specific grade-level indicators for the CCSS writing standards. Following is the listing for the grade 8 writing standards, as that is the upper limit of the considerations of this book. One can clearly see the elements for the three writing types and purposes delineated in the chart. The "top three" standards are supported by the remaining seven standards.

Writing is a skill that needs to grow and deepen for students over time. The manner in which students become better writers is to write often, write well, and write for a variety of purposes and audiences. The 10 Common Core State Standards for Writing are explicit, are detailed, and hold rigorous expectations for student performance.

CCSS Writing Standards: Grade 8

Source: Common Core State Standards (2010)

Text Types and Purposes

CCSS.ELA-Literacy.WR.8.1: Write arguments to support claims with clear reasons and relevant evidence.

a. Introduce claim(s), acknowledge and distinguish the claim(s) from alternate or opposing claims, and organize the reasons and evidence logically.

b. Support claim(s) with logical reasoning and relevant evidence, using accurate, credible sources and demonstrating an understanding of the topic or text.

c. Use words, phrases, and clauses to create cohesion and clarify the relationships among claim(s), counterclaims, reasons, and evidence.

d. Establish and maintain a formal style.

e. Provide a concluding statement or section that follows from and supports the argument presented.

CCSS.ELA-Literacy.WR.8.2: Write informative/explanatory texts to examine a topic and convey ideas, concepts, and information through the selection, organization, and analysis of relevant content.

a. Introduce a topic clearly, previewing what is to follow; organize ideas, concepts, and information into broader categories; include formatting (e.g., headings), graphics (e.g., charts, tables), and multimedia when useful to aiding comprehension.

b. Develop the topic with relevant, well-chosen facts, definitions, concrete details, quotations, or other information and examples.

c. Use appropriate and varied transitions to create cohesion and clarify the relationships among ideas and concepts.

d. Use precise language and domain-specific vocabulary to inform about or explain the topic.

e. Establish and maintain a formal style.

f. Provide a concluding statement or section that follows from and supports the information or explanation presented.

-continued

CCSS Writing Standards: Grade 8

Source: Common Core State Standards (2010)

CCSS.ELA-Literacy.WR.8.3: Write narratives to develop real or imagined experiences or events using effective technique, relevant descriptive details, and well-structured event sequences.

a. Engage and orient the reader by establishing a context and point of view and introducing a narrator and/or characters; organize an event sequence that unfolds naturally and logically.

b. Use narrative techniques, such as dialogue, pacing, description, and reflection, to develop experiences, events, and/or characters.

c. Use a variety of transition words, phrases, and clauses to convey sequence, signal shifts from one time frame or setting to another, and show the relationships among experiences and events.

d. Use precise words and phrases, relevant descriptive details, and sensory language to capture the action and convey experiences and events.

e. Provide a conclusion that follows from and reflects on the narrated experiences or events.

Production and Distribution of Writing

CCSS.ELA-Literacy.WR.8.4: Produce clear and coherent writing in which the development, organization, and style are appropriate to task, purpose, and audience. (Grade-specific expectations for writing types are defined in standards 1–3 above.)

CCSS.ELA-Literacy.WR.8.5: With some guidance and support from peers and adults, develop and strengthen writing as needed by planning, revising, editing, rewriting, or trying a new approach, focusing on how well purpose and audience have been addressed. (Editing for conventions should demonstrate command of Language standards 1–3 up to and including grade 8.)

CCSS.ELA-Literacy.WR.8.6: Use technology, including the Internet, to produce and publish writing and present the relationships between information and ideas efficiently as well as to interact and collaborate with others.

-continued

CCSS Writing Standards: Grade 8
Source: Common Core State Standards (2010)
Research to Build and Present Knowledge
CCSS.ELA-Literacy.WR.8.7: Conduct short research projects to answer a question (including a self-generated question), drawing on several sources and generating additional related, focused questions that allow for multiple avenues of exploration.
CCSS.ELA-Literacy.WR.8.8: Gather relevant information from multiple print and digital sources, using search terms effectively; assess the credibility and accuracy of each source; and quote or paraphrase the data and conclusions of others while avoiding plagiarism and following a standard format for citation.
CCSS.ELA-Literacy.WR.8.9: Draw evidence from literary or informational texts to support analysis, reflection, and research. a. Apply grade 8 Reading standards to literature (e.g., "Analyze how a modern work of fiction draws on themes, patterns of events, or character types from myths, traditional stories, or religious works such as the Bible, including describing how the material is rendered new"). b. Apply grade 8 Reading standards to literary nonfiction (e.g., "Delineate and evaluate the argument and specific claims in a text, assessing whether the reasoning is sound and the evidence is relevant and sufficient; recognize when irrelevant evidence is introduced").
Range of Writing
CCSS.ELA-Literacy.WR.8.10: Write routinely over extended time frames (time for research, reflection, and revision) and shorter time frames (a single sitting or a day or two) for a range of discipline-specific tasks, purposes, and audiences.

As teachers of elementary and middle grades, we need to teach our students to passionately engage with writing so that they can become the productive, creative, and prolific writers who constantly wish to learn more and intensify their relationship with the written word. There are many high-profile and/or high-salaried career opportunities that hinge on writing as the lifeline skill. Students should be hungry to reach beyond the mundane for their future goals. Being a strong writer with a powerful writing voice is a golden pairing.

The Classroom:
10 Practical Strategies on Quality Writing

1. Amplify student writing experiences. Students need dedicated instructional time to learn the skills and strategies necessary to become effective writers, as well as sufficient time to practice what they learn. For students to become proficient and sophisticated writers, they must engage in multiple writing opportunities and experiences.

The amount of time students spend writing needs to be increased significantly—with the time spent writing (really and truly writing) being doubled. This does not mean simply rearranging the number of daily minutes allocated to writing instruction. All teachers are well aware that the schedule for the school day cannot and will not expand operationally to accommodate this seismic shift.

It is suggested that all teachers at all grade levels and in all content areas take a reflective look at their existing activities, tasks, assignments, etc. and—within the parameters of the existing grade level and course schedules—change it up! Amplify writing instruction, incorporate more writing activities in learning centers, refocus routine writing tasks, reform class writing assignments and tasks to focus more on opinion/argument-based analyses, and transform mundane homework assignments into meaningful and complete writing projects.

The second part of this recommendation supports the idea that students who read more will become better writers. Teachers focusing their planned reading instruction on the goal of increasing text complexity will congruently support better writing. By reading complex literary and informational texts and initiating close reading, asking high-level, text-dependent questions as part of class discussions, and assessing reading through evidence-based responses, there will be much depth garnered from the experience. The reading and the discussion should spark connections to writing that students should be fervent to try. They will have a body of information to draw upon and insight into what others think. These connections through reading and responding should provide students with more matter to consider for writing. Students should be more prepared to write more deeply in a more informed way with more confidence.

Writing assignments will become the "connective tissue" to extend the reading processes in which students are immersed. Therefore, by substantially increasing (tripling!) your expectations for students' writing performance and providing opportune classroom activities, production and quality will incrementally deepen and proficiency will increase. The goal is to move students forward through the gradual release of responsibility framework into independence. At that level, students will be responding independently to a variety of writing tasks and generate and deliver substantive products routinely and across time.

2. Write out loud visually with students. Students need to see and hear experienced writers model great thinking about good writing and understand what skillful writers do as they write. Writing out loud permits teachers to verbalize the thinking behind the process as they construct a text type and write for a specific purpose.

Routman (2000) explains that "when writing aloud the teacher makes her thinking visible while composing and scribing in front of students. Students see a demonstration of how writing works—planning, thinking, drafting, organizing, selecting words, forming letters, spelling, punctuating, revising, editing, and formatting" (p. 33).

Writing aloud with visual aids (document viewer, interactive whiteboard, chart paper/markers) helps students visualize the formatting of quality writing elements and styles.

Teachers should plan to write out loud frequently for the types of writing that challenge students. As the writing is naturally occurring, students should pay close attention to explanations and demonstrations as the teacher actually constructs the text. The goal that is to be accomplished by the writing (offering point of view, challenging an opinion with different facts, etc.) will also be clear to students through explanations and models.

Repetition of the modeling by teachers provides oral and visual cues for students to better understand the processes. Making the writing process and writing structures visible to students is basic to improving their writing skills. Modeled writing will help them become more effective writers.

Modeling is not always a smooth, sequential process for students. It is not always fluid, whereby the students pick up on everything that the teacher is demonstrating. There is a level of "struggle" that needs to be considered, and the modeling needs to be ongoing so that students can improve over time.

Writing out loud often, becoming familiar with the required skills, and using the skills to create final products should better prepare students given the task, audience, and purpose.

3. Collaborate across the curriculum. Focus on your grade-level team or cross-curricula partners to initiate consistent practices for writing instruction across several subject areas. In some early grades, students may be in a self-contained classroom, with one teacher for the entire instructional day. The teacher is responsible for teaching all subjects. As students move up the grades, there may be configurations that have more than one teacher providing instruction to students. For instance, in some grades, students may switch classes just for reading and math. There might be two teachers that share responsibility for instruction in those two switched classrooms. Lastly, there might be grade levels in which students change classes every period. In this situation, multiple teachers might be responsible for instruction provided to one class of students.

Given the unique scheduling situations that prevail at various grade levels, opportunities for collaboration with another teacher or teachers are predictably possible. In most cases, there might be another teacher who teaches the same grade, if not the same subject. On occasion, it might be feasible to have students complete the same assignment in both classes. The two teachers could score their own classes' assignments, score the set of assignments completed by the other class, and then compare their results. If the assignment was clearly given, and there were specific criteria included in the project that explained what students were expected to produce, there should be parity between the two classes. This strategy can be used periodically to facilitate the scheduling. However, it can be helpful as it gives teachers data from other students to which they can better assess their assigned students' performance and progress.

Also for the sake of consistency, teachers can collaborate on structures, formats, procedures, rubrics, etc. so that there is instructional coherence across the grade-level classrooms. Writing essays in social studies class should not take a different form or be rated differently from an essay assessed by the English language arts/literacy teacher. The same graphic organizers, semantic maps, scoring rubrics, and grading practices can also be utilized so that students understand the equity across classrooms. By using shared tools and resources, and by focusing on similar procedural elements, students will quickly see the "blurring" of the lines beyond each classroom's wall and become more familiar more quickly with the procedures they must follow and criteria used in multiple classes. They will then hopefully have more time to focus and concentrate on the products they are responsible for developing rather than on the disparate procedural elements. Similarly, one assignment might cross several classes and be graded "to count" in several different subjects.

There are many instructional strategies that can be agreed upon by the group as initial undertakings so that there is great consistency in the practices in which students will be engaged. This includes writing formats, graphic organizers, annotation guides, rubrics to formatively assess students, learning centers, and grading consistencies.

Once management tools are shared, the team needs to focus on how the curriculum can support interdisciplinary connections, especially in writing. Units of study, extended performance tasks, assignments for content-based readings, assignments counting for grades in more than one class based on rubric elements, etc. can also be considered for swift implementation so that there is cohesion and consistency. The message here is that writing in the content-area classes needs to increase.

4. Writing with the technologies. The summative ELA assessments permeating the educational landscape require skill and proficiency in writing—beyond the composition of the text. Skill with the technology tools needs to be improved and intensified.

Students should practice using a computer when completing written tasks—throughout the writing process. With a computer, text can be added, deleted, and moved easily. Furthermore, students can access tools, such as the spell-checker and thesaurus, to enhance their written compositions. Platforms and templates to assist with writing should match the templates designed for assessments.

As with any technology, teachers should guide students on proper use of the computer and any relevant programs before students compose independently. It's suggested that online repositories (Google Drive, Dropbox) are set up for students to save and share their work with the teacher, who may access the written products to assess, provide feedback, and/or grade.

5. Analyze student writing samples as a grade-level professional learning community (PLC). Collaborating with a group of educators as part of a professional learning community (PLC) can help to analyze the effectiveness of the educational activities designed for student learning. Teachers who collaboratively analyze student work products learn to consistently use tools (rubrics) and form mutual agreements (performance levels) so that there is inter-rater reliability among all the constituents as they work to improve student achievement over time through the use of evidence.

This collaboration broadens the perspective of looking at student work samples across all the participating teachers' classes—not just looking at one's own class in isolation. Teachers consider the following questions:

- What strengths do my students have with the required knowledge and skills?
- What student learning needs still are apparent with the required knowledge and skills?
- Do my students have adequate foundational content to proceed with new learning?
- Do my students have requisite process skills to proceed with new learning?
- How can I support student learning through scaffolding? Differentiation? Interventions?

The most important benefit of analyzing student work is improved student learning. Teachers also gain greater clarity about outcomes.

6. Create super sentences. Creating super sentences by combining simple sentences is a straightforward task to design and implement. Teachers explicitly instruct students to write more complex and sophisticated sentences. This process is not as simple as combining two short sentences together into one longer sentence. Teachers should model how to combine two or more related sentences so that they create a more complex sentence.

Here are two simple and short sentences:

My dad wants to get a new job.

He is preparing for job interviews.

It is not acceptable to just combine them in to one longer sentence: *My dad wants to get a new job, and he is preparing for job interviews.*

The finished product seeks to have complex sentences constructed that include pumped-up vocabulary and the possible addition of clauses, content, unique thoughts, and sophisticated language inclusive of Tier Two words.

For example:

My father is presently preparing for job interviews by rewriting his résumé; his career goal is to land an upper-management position for a Fortune 500 company that is rewarding and has job security.

Students practice the skill and follow along with the modeling. They skim their writing products to locate potential sentences that can be combined. They apply these sentence-creation skills as they write or revise their own writing products. The thinking, revising, and editing process could entail several cycles so that there is progression in the development of better complex sentences.

7. Participate in student writing competitions, essay contests, and poetry recitals. Based on the type of writing being produced in the classroom, teachers should seek out venues for writing forums, story competitions, essay contests, poetry festivals, and the like. All of these opportunities may not require the submission of written work for award purposes. Student writing can also be submitted for consideration as part of a panel discussion of a public forum on a topic of interest, whereby the students present their prepared written products.

Traditional competitions are also a way for students to be acknowledged for quality work. Many professional organizations and civic groups host competitions annually to which students can submit their writing pieces and possibly receive awards.

8. Form a writers' collaborative to facilitate student-with-student conferencing. Students make great cheerleaders for other students, and they themselves benefit from the process of supporting a classmate. Forming a writers' collaborative would be voluntary on the part of the student participants. The idea would be for them to collaborate throughout the writing process by brainstorming ideas about a topic, responding to drafts in a small writing group, or helping peers edit or revise their work. The writers' collaborative could be scheduled outside of class time or as an in-class activity. Working collaboratively advances the skills of all of the participants exponentially, and their support for each other's work builds confidence individually as well as collectively.

The writers' collaborative also can expand to include collaborative writing, whereby two or more students jointly develop a single text. Joint authorship promotes negotiation skills, consensus building, ability to schedule work, and shared responsibility for the completion of the written product. Students can collaborate by publishing a weekly newsletter or an online class newspaper, starting a community campaign for a student-identified problem to be solved, or composing stories to share with their friends or classmates.

9. Publish students' writing to extend the audience beyond the classroom. When students understand that their work will be published in the real-world domain, they know an audience will see it and will therefore work harder and smarter. Additionally, the quality of the work produced is often more meaningful and polished.

Many reputable sites that will host students' written works exist online. Sites for which there are submission criteria for student work pieces to be considered are also present. Most importantly, local solutions abound to ease into this practice at a classroom and/or school level. As a beginning step, publishing can take a variety of forms, including displaying student work prominently in the classroom.

Most schools have a website. Without much difficulty, a section of the website could be designed as a gallery to host student work samples. Identifying information could be eliminated so that only the work itself is shared publicly.

Another way to publish student work is to have students create their own published books, individually and as a class project, and have the books professionally bound. Having students produce real books has great benefits and, given the technology resources freely available, it is definitely an achievable undertaking. Self-publishing is very popular for adults, and the same procedures can be replicated for student products. Student books can be disseminated in the school library, at school functions, and to benefactors who wish to purchase a copy.

Students who successfully publish a book can receive credit for their accomplishment by the school holding official book-signing sessions at which the student author can engage with others and discuss the storyline, the solution put forth, or the characters and their development. The student can elaborate on the author's purpose and the meaning. This connection to public speaking imitates a real-life specialized event and has long-lasting meaning for students.

10. Use *In Common: Effective Writing for All Students—K–12* student writing samples. Teachers have been asking for actual student writing samples from the summative ELA assessments aligned to national and/or state standards to use as models for writing instruction in their classrooms. Now that the summative ELA assessments require students to provide extended written narrative and analytical responses after having read and interacted with text, new exemplars of student writings need to be made available as models of quality writing. Sources that can provide these samples will meet the needs of many teachers.

In Common: Effective Writing for All Students is a valuable resource that was developed through collaboration with The Vermont Writing Collaborative, Student Achievement Partners, and the Council of Chief State School Officers. The resulting body of work represents a multitude of authentic student writing samples that have been collected from schools across the United States, compiled for grades K–12 by grade level, organized by writing mode, and annotated.

In addition to the student samples, the writing prompts and source documents (informational text passages) have been included so that interested teachers can replicate the tasks in their classrooms. The student samples are intended to represent examples of quality writing at each grade level, not benchmark papers. There are annotations provided for each paper that can inform the connection to instructional standards and objectives.

According to the *In Common* user's guide (p. 10):

- The files are organized into three sections by writing types (argument/opinion, informative/explanatory, and narrative) and by grade cluster (K–2, 3–5, 6–12).

- There are at least two samples of student work (and often many more) provided at each grade level.

- Each piece is in a separate, downloadable file, freely available for classroom use and professional development.

In Common is accessible from the Student Achievement Partners' website.

Online Resources for Extending Learning

- ASCD—Association for Supervision and Curriculum Development offers online access to an extensive catalog of free resources that empower educators to support literacy success. *Educational Leadership*, its monthly online journal, provides up-to-date research and resources in professional development, capacity building, and educational leadership.

- International Literacy Association (formerly International Reading Association)—Publishes cutting-edge research on literacy and translates the research into practical resources for educators and students.

- National Writing Project—A network of sites connecting colleges and universities that provides teachers with resources and research to improve the teaching of writing.

- ReadWriteThink—A partnership between the International Literacy Association and the National Council of Teachers of English. This site offers literacy resources by grade level. Lesson plans, strategy guides, videos, and professional development resources are available.

- ReadWriteThink Stapleless Book—Students interact with a simple interface of several templates to produce and print their own eight-page book just by folding and cutting. It is available from the ReadWriteThink website.

- *Stone Soup* magazine—Publishes original, creative writing (stories and poems) by children ages eight to 13.

Summary

The writing tasks on the summative ELA assessments aligned to national and/or state standards vary by design, are different in purpose, exude rigor, target a specific audience, and are directly connected to the prompt provided. The writing tasks are designed to assess students' skills and abilities to develop, organize, and express information and ideas in a manner appropriate to the task, the audience, and the purpose. The tasks are challenging in that they mesh with grade-level reading passages and media clips, which students must be able to read successfully and use as the springboard for their writing. At the same time, students must analyze and examine the reading passages and media clips for evidence to support their position and enhance their thinking as they execute their positional response.

On the assessments, students will write for varying time frames for a range of tasks—some short writing scenarios and some extended. For instance, writing a narrative may be done in a shorter allocated time frame than writing an opinion/argument essay. As educators, we need to think about how to support students in learning various writing response styles so they can learn to produce final writing pieces of differing styles, lengths, and genres.

Since the assessments are being delivered in an online, computer-based format, students will engage with technology-based processes and tools to produce, revise, edit, and publish their written responses. As writing instructors, we must look to enhance students' facility with writing using technology and ensure that they can manipulate technology to their advantage in order to produce a quality written response online in the time allocated.

As we unpack the information surrounding the writing tasks, it is imperative that we focus on creating exemplary writers, in the same way we need to create prolific readers. Quality instruction by highly qualified educators who model strategic writing practices will help students link the reading-writing connection solidly with their work. We can make good writers better and, at the same time, make writing a newly acquired proficiency for those who might be struggling. Since this is all new at this moment in time, we need to seize the opportunity to fashion the plan we have to improve students' writing capabilities so they can be ready for the next goal.

CHAPTER 5:
Integrating Content from Diverse Media Formats as Text; Understanding and Analyzing Data Visually and Quantitatively

Chapters 1 through 4 elaborate on the knowledge, skills, and dispositions students must possess to exhibit proficiency in literacy, in the broadest sense. All of the elemental skills across the spectrum of reading, writing, and speaking and listening coalesce into shaping the essence of a literate individual. This development enables students to become critical thinkers, complex problem-solvers, and quality producers. This chapter examines the set of skills modern learners need. The focus is on how these skills integrate into the larger literacy picture.

Information, media, and technology influence our daily lives in a profound way. The speed, volume, and diversity of information touch points with which we must interact efficiently and effectively are mind-boggling. The Internet, our cell phones, our e-mail accounts, infomercials, telemarketers, etc. bombard us daily and simultaneously. A multitude of stories, news events, financial offers, advertisements, educational opportunities, and shopping bargains are always calling out to us. All of these require our quick attention to, and astute evaluation of, the information to determine if the facts are accurate, the sources are credible, and the information is believable. Mistruths and scams are pervasive, and only our skillfulness and our critical-thinking skills keep us from making wrong decisions. Some decisions could impact us significantly and far into our futures. Identity theft, online postings, e-mail tracking, etc. have personal, financial, and professional implications for which we need to understand the outcomes and consequences. As citizens, and as modern consumers, we need to be able to read, interpret, and evaluate visual and digital information critically and competently.

The Partnership for 21st Century Skills (2011) presents a framework representing "a holistic view of 21st-century teaching and learning" on its website that "combines discrete focus on 21st-century student outcomes (a blending of specific skills, content knowledge, expertise, and literacies) with innovative support systems to help students master the multi-dimensional abilities required of them in the 21st century and beyond."

As educators, we must impart to students the same analysis, evaluation, and management skills we continue to perfect to deal with handling the overabundance and intrusion of this perpetual flood of information. Students must internalize these key understandings and critical life skills through our teaching, much practice, and their learning.

The information presented to us visually and digitally through media can be categorized as informational text. It is presented to us as "text" in differing formats. This type of text can be represented in many forms—including data represented graphically in tables, graphs, diagrams, charts, etc.—in reading and writing contexts.

Students in grades 3–8 should demonstrate skill in "reading" this specialized form of text. They also must be adept at analyzing this type of informational data represented in graphical form. Elementary students should be able to communicate the results of the analysis in written form, following the expected levels of performance for their grade level.

This chapter explores how teachers can provide students with opportunities to integrate and evaluate content presented through diverse media and various formats. There is also a focus on inferencing.

Making inferences is implied throughout this chapter and is a prerequisite skill to meeting the intended learning expectations for success at every grade level in literacy and on the summative ELA assessments. One of the expectations of the College and Career Readiness Anchor Standards for Reading is for students to "Read closely to determine what the text says explicitly and to make logical inferences from it; and cite specific evidence from the text when writing or speaking to support conclusions drawn from the text" (CCR Standard 1, National Center for Best Practices and Council of Chief State School Officers, 2010).

This chapter looks at text from a broad view, which includes all graphical, digital, and media formats, as well as other types of visualizations. These other visualizations include artwork, photographs, and political cartoons. This chapter introduces how these elements will be portrayed and used on the national summative ELA assessments. Furthermore, this chapter discusses inferencing skills and applying them to visual and digital formats and graphical representations. The chapter closes with some online sites that provide resources for teachers.

Summative Assessments: What to Expect

Focus on Diverse Media Formats as Text

The summative ELA assessments will incorporate media representations of literary works as well as visual and graphical representations of informational text. They will be paired with traditional text passages. The media format that "texts" will take include video clips, audio clips, podcasts, drama productions, political cartoons, graphics, and so on.

Students, beginning in grade 3, will be expected to comprehend each "text" and answer several text-dependent questions about each piece to determine comprehension. They will also be asked to engage possibly in one or more of the following tasks when they are working with literature or informational "texts":

- compare literary elements, including theme;
- compare central ideas, topics (including same event and point of view) in two or more "texts";
- compare and/or analyze different versions of the same "text";
- compare main ideas and/or topics, including the same event or point of view;
- analyze how ideas are transformed from one "text" to another.

(Partnership for the Assessment of Readiness for College and Careers, 2015, pp. 6–12)

Here is an example of a possible summative assessment writing task. Remember, students will always provide an extended written response only after having read, viewed, or listened to "texts." The writing is in response to the reading and often takes the form of an analytic essay.

Example:

- Analyze _____, the main character from the passage in the book _____. (The assessment will provide the segment of the selection.)
- Compare him/her to the character in the audio and film versions of the same book. (The audio and video clips will also be provided.)
- Using evidence from all three sources, write an analytic essay that reveals two ways in which the character is similar in all three pieces and two ways the character is different. Provide specific textual evidence to support your statements.

Focus on Understanding and Analyzing Data Visually and Quantitatively

Jan V. White (1984) in his seminal book, *Using Charts and Graphs: 1,000 Ideas for Visual Persuasion*, tells us that "just as mathematical expressions are a language, graphics, too, are a form of communication. Charts, graphs, diagrams, and tables are all statements combining several thoughts into a related format, just as language is composed of infinitely arrangeable words, so is its graphic counterpart. Your thoughts—your message—make you choose words and their arrangement when you speak. You may choose to say it simply, embroider it with verbal embellishment, symbolize it in poetic form, or even put it in Latin if you think that will communicate best. And so it is with graphics. You can arrange a collection of statistics in a visual format that corresponds to a simple statement, a flowery rodomontade, a poem, or something with a foreign flavor to it. You can even tell lies if you want to" (p. x).

Another feature of the summative ELA assessments is the inclusion of informational graphics, which students must interpret and/or relate to the content of the passage. The ability to understand and analyze quantitative information and ideas expressed graphically in tables, graphs, charts, etc. is an essential skill for college- and career-ready students.

Even though this was written more than 30 years ago, the information quoted by White (1984) is even more pertinent today. He elaborates that "Nowadays, wherever we look, we see evidence of the importance of charts and graphs in communication. Practically every advertisement for computer hardware shows a little screen with graphics on it as proof that computers can do it better. We also see charts and graphs used ever more cunningly in the pages of consumer magazines when, not too long ago, they were only to be found in specialized publications dealing with economics, the sciences, and business. Charts have catapulted from the stock market pages into every other section of today's newspapers to illustrate (and prove) trends of all kinds. They appear on television as credible proofs of someone's (anyone's) claims, and no 'presentation' is deemed complete without some attempt, however primitive, at visual leavening. In sum, the day of visual statistics is upon us, and we ought to make the most of it" (p. 1).

On the summative ELA assessments, students will be expected to discern factual information and evidence from the text, with the text being a graphical representation or visualization. Students will need to be able to "read" the graph and cite evidence from it to support a position. The graphical representation could be just one of two or more texts that students will need to compare in order to complete an extended written response.

Focus on Technology-Enhanced Response Modes

The summative ELA assessments are being administered in an online environment with computers as the means of administration. Logistically, it supports the viability of implementing 21st-century skills. This online platform also provides innovative ways for questions to be asked and answers to be provided.

There are new types of questions that embrace the ease provided through the technologies. Technology-enhanced selected response questions feature drag-and-drop, highlighting, scrolling, and sequencing. These skills are not difficult. Students should find the tactile aspects required to complete these technology-enhanced questions somewhat appealing and interesting given that they replicate students' on-screen response modes used to play online games, send e-mails, etc. The skills are layered to enhance the engagement of students and also measure skills that were not measurable through a pencil-paper test.

Let us now turn to different ways that students can analyze content.

What Is Graphical Data?

Graphical data is a method of delivering information using a picture, or graphic, to display or communicate information or intent. Today, business professionals refer to graphical data in terms of "infographics."

What Is Inferencing?

Inferencing is defined as "the act or process of reaching a conclusion about something from known facts or evidence; a conclusion or opinion that is formed because of known facts or evidence" (*Merriam-Webster*, 2015). Students are also being asked to make inferences online.

Reading Rockets (2015) provides us with a more practical understanding of inferencing on its website: "Observations occur when we can see something happening. In contrast, inferences are what we figure out based on an experience. Helping students understand when information is implied, or not directly stated, will improve their skill in drawing conclusions and making inferences. These skills will be needed for all sorts of school assignments, including reading, science, and social studies. Inferential thinking is a complex skill that will develop over time and with experience."

Good readers use many strategies to infer. These include word/text clues, picture clues, defining unknown words, predicting, asking reflective questions, looking for emotions (feelings), drawing conclusions, and connecting background knowledge to the text.

"Inferences are not stated explicitly in the passage. Rather, inference questions require readers to draw conclusions from the factual knowledge or evidence presented. In order to answer an inference question, readers must understand the logic of the author's statements and decide what is or is not reasonable. Inference questions are as much about critical thinking as they are about critical reading" (MassBay Community College Academic Achievement Center, 2005, p. 4).

Inferencing is a comprehension skill and a critical skill that students are explicitly taught in the English language arts/literacy classroom from the earliest grades onward. On the summative ELA assessments, students are asked inferencing questions in a clear and straightforward manner. Here is a hypothetical example of a third-grade ELA practice assessment that would be completed in an online format.

Example:

The test-taker has just read a passage that describes the relationship between two boys who live in the same seaport village and enjoy playing soccer, going to school, and flying colorful kites. The first question of the series asks:

Part A

"What inference can be made about Amir's relationship with José?"

(The student would type a response into the box below.)

Part B

"Support your answer with details from the passage. Highlight two sentences in the passage that support your answer in Part A."

Students are then asked to answer a Part B question in which they must provide evidence from the text to support the answer they selected in the first question. They would actually highlight the two sentences in the passage.

Inferencing skills now need to connect beyond the written page and be focused on the visual aspects of our world and all that we visually and digitally "read" on a daily basis. In many cases, what we read is in chart forms, diagrams, graphs, etc. The ability to make inferences and predictions based on data is a critical skill students need to develop.

Integrating Content from Diverse Media Formats as Text

Today's textbooks and educational resources for students are very visual in nature; they are not just pages of linear text. On almost every page in a textbook, there is a photograph, a picture, a diagram, a chart, or a map. We assume that students understand how to decipher information from the visual representations. How do we really know that they are getting the full benefit of the author's intent? We don't.

Some students come to the information intuitively. Others need explicit instruction and practice to extract information from a visual. Think about this question: Why do authors of books structure information in graphs or charts instead of writing several sentences of text on the page to explain what they are thinking or want to show? We explore the answer to this question in the next few pages.

Understanding and Analyzing Data Visually and Quantitatively

Understanding data involves being able to interpret the meaning of the data collected, organized, and displayed in the form of a table, a bar chart, a line graph, or another representation. As teachers provide instruction in the process of analyzing data, they need to emphasize that it involves what these patterns might mean. TeacherVision (2015) provides an informative list of the types of graphs and their best use.

- Bar graph: Compares various items or ideas.
- Histogram: Shows frequency and compares items or ideas; each bar represents an interval of values.
- Line graph: Shows change over time.
- Pictograph: Shows frequency and compares items or ideas.
- Circle graph (or pie graph): Shows parts or percentages of a whole.

Students, knowing which graph type makes the most sense for specific tasks, can answer questions more easily when analyzing data if they are familiar with the graph's purpose. The telling question that should underlie teachers' lessons and instructional activities is: What do students have to know so that this visual makes sense to them and they understand it? Examining the visual or graphical representation, questions need to be asked of students so that they can connect the dots more closely together, gather information, and draw a conclusion about the visual. How involved a teacher gets into the analysis and the terms he/she uses depends on the grade level of the students and the purpose of the task.

Probing questions that could be asked include:

- What pattern do you see?
- What does this visual graph tell you? Can you summarize what you see?
- What elements are critical for understanding? Images? Headings? Text?
- What does it not say? What key pieces of information are missing?
- What does it mean? Why does it matter?
- Who could use this data? How could they use it?
- Why is this data shown in this type of graph?
- What questions do you have? What more do you need to know?
- Do you think the information is true? Correct? Accurate?
- Can you offer an opinion about the correctness and credibility of the information?
- Can you provide three reasons why you would support this view? Three reasons why you can't?
- Would you use this information to make an important decision? Why or why not?

When graphs and charts are embedded in text, as text, the author uses them deliberately to provide crucial information to the reader that is difficult to obtain in any other way.

Teachers can use writing to augment instruction in other subject areas. For example, if students are learning to interpret graphs in math, teachers can present students with a graph from a recent newspaper and ask them to write a paragraph about what the graph is trying to convey. This exercise encourages students to think carefully about how effectively the graph conveys information, and at the same time, it gives students an opportunity to apply and practice writing strategies and skills.

Common Core and Integrating Content from Diverse Media Formats as Text

According to the Common Core State Standards, all students are expected to be involved with understanding and analyzing data in such a way that it adds to their body of knowledge. College and Career Readiness Standard 7 for Reading is based in the "Integration of Knowledge and Ideas" and focuses deftly on diverse media formats and connections to literature and informational text. Additionally, this standard goes beyond the simple expectation of interpreting quantitative information through number responses and moves to data analysis. This degree of analysis fosters higher-level evaluation by having students write about what they uncovered through questioning, evidence from the text, and making predictions.

The use of digital media plays a prominent role in connecting literature (fiction and literary nonfiction) to other genres beyond books. Digital representations using books on tape, video clips, audio clips, podcasts, webinars, TED talks, etc. are used to provide students sufficient and appropriate interactions with multiple texts.

The following charts clearly identify the skills and activities that students should progressively master as they achieve success in their grade level for the literary standards, the informational text standards, and the subject-related standards in history/social studies, science, and technical subjects.

Reading: Literature—Integration of Knowledge and Ideas	
Source: Common Core State Standards (2010)	
CCR Anchor Standard 7: Integrate and evaluate content presented in diverse media and formats, including visually and quantitatively, as well as in words.	
Grade	**Grade-Specific Standard**
Grade 3	Explain how specific aspects of a text's illustrations contribute to what is conveyed by the words in a story (e.g., create mood, emphasize aspects of a character or setting). (CCSS.ELA-Literacy.RL.3.7)
Grade 4	Make connections between the text of a story or drama and a visual or oral presentation of the text, identifying where each version reflects specific descriptions and directions in the text. (CCSS.ELA-Literacy.RL.4.7)
Grade 5	Analyze how visual and multimedia elements contribute to the meaning, tone, or beauty of a text (e.g., graphic novel, multimedia presentation of fiction, folktale, myth, poem). (CCSS.ELA-Literacy.RL.5.7)
Grade 6	Compare and contrast the experience of reading a story, drama, or poem to listening to or viewing an audio, video, or live version of the text, including contrasting what they "see" and "hear" when reading the text to what they perceive when they listen or watch. (CCSS.ELA-Literacy.RL.6.7)
Grade 7	Compare and contrast a written story, drama, or poem to its audio, filmed, staged, or multimedia version, analyzing the effects of techniques unique to each medium (e.g., lighting, sound, color, or camera focus and angles in a film). (CCSS.ELA-Literacy.RL.7.7)
Grade 8	Analyze the extent to which a filmed or live production of a story or drama stays faithful to or departs from the text or script, evaluating the choices made by the director or actors. (CCSS.ELA-Literacy.RL.8.7)

Reading: Informational Text—Integration of Knowledge and Ideas

Source: Common Core State Standards (2010)

CCR Anchor Standard 7: Integrate and evaluate content presented in diverse media and formats, including visually and quantitatively, as well as in words.	
Grade	**Grade-Specific Standard**
Grade 3	Use information gained from illustrations (e.g., maps, photographs) and the words in a text to demonstrate understanding of the text (e.g., where, when, why, and how key events occur). (CCSS.ELA-Literacy.RI.3.7)
Grade 4	Interpret information presented visually, orally, or quantitatively (e.g., in charts, graphs, diagrams, time lines, animations, or interactive elements on Web pages) and explain how the information contributes to an understanding of the text in which it appears. (CCSS.ELA-Literacy.RI.4.7)
Grade 5	Draw on information from multiple print or digital sources, demonstrating the ability to locate an answer to a question quickly or to solve a problem efficiently. (CCSS.ELA-Literacy.RI.5.7)
Grade 6	Integrate information presented in different media or formats (e.g., visually, quantitatively) as well as in words to develop a coherent understanding of a topic or issue. (CCSS.ELA-Literacy.RI.6.7)
Grade 7	Compare and contrast a text to an audio, video, or multimedia version of the text, analyzing each medium's portrayal of the subject (e.g., how the delivery of a speech affects the impact of the words). (CCSS.ELA-Literacy.RI.7.7)
Grade 8	Evaluate the advantages and disadvantages of using different mediums (e.g., print or digital text, video, multimedia) to present a particular topic or idea. (CCSS.ELA-Literacy.RI.8.7)

This chart represents the grades 6–8 literacy standards for history/social studies, science, and technical subjects. One can readily see that students will be engaged with primary sources, foundational documents, and technical texts through visualizations, flowcharts, graphs, and other digital resources like audio clips of famous speeches, historical representations on video, etc. Teachers in the subject-area content classes must embed the use of digital media into their lessons and class activities on a regular basis.

Reading Standards for Literacy in History/Social Studies, Science, and Technical Subjects		
Source: Common Core State Standards (2010)		
	Reading Standards for Literacy in History/Social Studies	**Reading Standards for Literacy in Science and Technical Subjects**
CCR Anchor Standard 7: Integrate and evaluate content presented in diverse media and formats, including visually and quantitatively, as well as in words.		
Grade Band	**Grade-Band-Specific Standard**	
Grades 6–8	Integrate visual information (e.g., in charts, graphs, photographs, videos, or maps) with other information in print and digital texts. (CCSS.ELA-Literacy. RH.6–8.7)	Integrate quantitative or technical information expressed in words in a text with a version of that information expressed visually (e.g., in a flowchart, diagram, model, graph, or table). (CCSS.ELA-Literacy.RST.6–8.7)

There is a notable connection between this concept of integrating content from diverse media formats as text and understanding and analyzing data visually and quantitatively in the "Research to Build and Present Knowledge" writing standards.

The Classroom:
10 Practical Strategies on Integrating Content from Diverse Media Formats as Text

1. Read advertisements with a critical eye. Every day, television, magazine, and newspaper advertisements tout what a great product the advertiser is promoting. Students need to practice critical-thinking skills, and advertisements are a great source of data. What does "four out of five dentists" really mean? Teachers can enlarge the written ad by placing it on a document viewer and have students challenge the data.

These advertisements may not be in graphical form (chart, graph, etc.). Students are looking for data to be embedded in the text. Students should read the advertisement carefully and examine the data. They will have to read the advertisement to uncover what the data really means.

This activity is a preliminary activity to the next strategy. In this next strategy, students will practice with visual graphics.

2. Practice, practice, practice to interpret visual representations with ease. Teachers should incorporate numerous and frequent opportunities for students to practice viewing graphs, charts, diagrams, and other forms of visual representations. At first, teachers should provide a list of key questions that can guide student practice. As students become more proficient, they can add their own questions to the list. Students should discuss these graphical representations in pairs, in small groups, and as a whole class. A variety of writing activities should be constructed, and students should be expected to write about their findings as a culminating activity.

Another component of this strategy is enlisting students in locating interesting, authentic visual and graphical images from newspapers, magazines, business reports, and student newsletters (Scholastic, *Weekly Reader*, etc.). The analysis would follow the same process.

This strategy works equally well for representations that accurately reflect the data for which the visual was based as it does for poorly-constructed, inaccurate samples. The responses generated by the students about the inaccuracy, incorrectness, and unreliability of the poorly-constructed visuals are most often the best learning resource.

3. Foster graphics literacy in the classroom through collaboration with the math and science teachers. English language arts/literacy teachers cannot assume total responsibility for students mastering the skills related to graphic literacy. Enlist the support and collaboration of the math and science teachers at your grade level. Work with them to teach elements of graphing and the content-specific vocabulary. On a regular basis, have students construct graphical representations of things occurring in real life. By constructing their own graphs, students will strengthen their understanding of how graphs are constructed and the information that is garnered from using graphs. Students should repeat this a number of times and create different types of graphs—circle graphs, bar graphs, etc. In this way, they will also understand that the type of graph must be suitable for the data being presented.

4. Learn about types of graphs and charts. People who use graphs use common names for various types of graphs. Students should become familiar with the graph types and proficient in how they are properly applied to data. Common graph types are: line graph, bar graph, pictograph, pie chart, organization chart, flowchart, bubble chart, stacked column chart (stacked bar graph), histogram, and scatterplot.

5. Build academic vocabulary. Students will be expected to speak and write to convey what they have learned through the analysis of graphical visualizations. Teachers need to provide vocabulary instruction in the Tier Three specialized vocabulary words and correct statistical terms so students have the words necessary to clearly convey their thinking. Terms, such as axis, range, median, correlation, interval, and so on, should become part of their vocabulary.

6. Analyze political cartoons with the "Cartoon Analysis Checklist." Political cartoons are visual representations. They are primary sources that history and social studies teachers can use to make learning more dramatic and fun for students. They represent opinions.

According to Jonathan Burack, in his article "Interpreting Political Cartoons in the History Classroom" (2010), "the cartoons offer intriguing and entertaining insights into the public mood, the underlying cultural assumptions of an age, and attitudes toward key events or trends of the times."

Most history textbooks still include political cartoons. Teachers need to concentrate on their power in having students uncover a great deal of content information, symbolism, irony, and academic vocabulary. Students need to be taught how to understand the political cartoons in their daily newspaper.

The "Cartoon Analysis Checklist" (Burack, 2010) can be downloaded from the National History Education Clearinghouse website. This resource guides students in developing skills in reading political cartoons so they use them effectively.

The checklist includes definitions and examples of several core concepts with accompanying activities. Each concept is listed here and a key activity can be found on the site as well as background information that sets the stage and gives students information critical to the process of completing the task.

- Symbol and metaphor
- Visual distortion
- Irony in words and images
- Stereotype and caricature
- An argument, not a slogan
- The uses and misuses of political cartoons

7. Diversify the media modes for literature-based texts. Teachers can have students experience the reading of a story, drama, or poem as it was originally meant to be enjoyed. Students can also experience listening to or viewing an audio, video, or live version of the same story, drama, or poem. When students have access to a variety of modalities, teachers should encourage students to compare and contrast the experiences. Focusing on contrasting what they "hear" and "see" when reading the text to what they perceive when they listen or watch will help to support the learning.

8. Let great speakers come alive. Teachers should encourage students to interact with great historians, politicians, religious figures, actors, etc. This activity works in any content classroom and connects students directly to the curriculum goals. Students should read the text of a significant speech as a close reading activity with multiple readings. Students then listen to an audio, video, or multimedia version of the text, analyzing each medium's portrayal of the subject (e.g., how the delivery of a speech affects the impact of the words). There are online sites that have archives of speeches throughout history available for downloading in which the original orator is actually giving the speech. Students get to hear history come alive through voices from the past.

9. Change it up! Adjust instructional activities to include a focus on multimedia and digital media. As part of every lesson, teachers should commit to including at least one newly created multimedia, digital media, or graphical visualization activity. This will cause teachers to modify and expand their professional choices into activities in alignment with the summative ELA assessments.

10. Create graphical stories. Creating descriptive stories from graphs that have no identifying words engages students in logical thinking. The graphical representations do not refer to mathematical data but rely on details from the charts to support students in their thinking and development of the story.

Online Resources for Extending Learning

- Discovery Education—Teacher guides for social studies and studying tables, charts, and diagrams that are downloadable for use in classrooms.

- Oliphant's Anthem: Pat Oliphant at the Library of Congress—Features numerous works of the 1966 Pulitzer Prize-winning editorial cartoonist Pat Oliphant.

- The Open University—OpenLearn, the home of free learning from The Open University, offers a free online course entitled "Diagrams, Charts, and Graphs." This course teaches how to interpret these tools and use them to convey information effectively.

- Oregon Department of Education—Sample summative items for teachers in ELA for grades 3–5, 6–8, and 9–11. Subject areas include reading, writing, speaking/listening, and research.

- Public domain images of charts and graphs—Thousands of free images can be downloaded and used for classroom problem-solving and interpretation. These are visual representations that tell a story and represent trends, information, etc. that students can review, interpret, and analyze. Students can also write original stories about their graph or chart.

- Public domain political cartoons—Free downloadable images of political cartoons are available for use in classrooms to correspond with history/social studies lessons and historical time periods, events, and issues.

- Using Charts and Graphs: 1,000 Ideas for Visual Persuasion—Jan V. White's book is available for download in the public domain. It is 220 pages showcasing examples of the work of this chapter.

- Virginia Department of Education: Standards of Learning (SOL) Practice Items—There is an extensive bank of Technology-Enhanced Items (TEI) online for elementary, middle, and high school in math, science, reading, and writing. Item types include drag and drop, hot spots, graphs, and fill-in-the-blank.

Summary

Chapter 5 exemplifies the connections to reality as we are living it today. Scroll through the text on our multiple devices—laptops, tablets, and smartphones. Flip through today's magazines and newspapers. Open your personal and professional e-mails, and glance through the traditional mail you receive at home.

What appears on our screens and in front of our faces represents diverse media formats and features an overwhelming amount of visual information and graphical representations. We consume a great deal of informational text, and the format of that text is visual. Graphical representations are used frequently in television, newspapers, and online advertisements to solicit our attention because the format allows a tremendous amount of information to be delivered in a succinct, yet very effective and appealing, format.

When we think about the ways that we understand the world around us, we are constantly manipulating visual and graphical text. When we book an airline ticket, purchase theater tickets, order a new pair of shoes, or check out the best new car to purchase, we are always seeking ways to compare prices, find the best deal, negotiate with a variety of sources, arrange the fastest delivery, etc. There are always graphs and charts, star ratings, etc. directing us to the next step and our final choices. On a daily basis, we are constantly leveraging visual and graphical data.

Through these processes, we are integrating math with literacy, health with art, and science with technology, and we are synthesizing it all into being an educated citizen.

This list could go on forever. As we prepare our students to live their best lives, opportunities for learning need to model the encounters students experience in the real world. That is the foundational rationale underpinning the administration of the summative ELA assessments aligned to national and/or state standards online. Technology is being used for the first time by millions of students, beginning in the third grade. Imagine what we have accomplished with this feat! Yes, there have been technology issues, but the overwhelming success of this catalytic change will forever prevail in the way assessments will be administered to students. There is no going back. We will continue to get better at moving forward.

Given this innovative administration platform, these technology-forward assessments offer new possibilities in the types of questions, tasks, simulations, and problems that can be designed and incorporated at all grade levels.

Students need to be critical readers of visual and graphical representations. They need to be able to read and analyze data as efficiently as they read a text passage. They need to interact with diverse media formats in instructional settings. They need to view and listen to data presented orally, listen for bias, separate truth from falsehoods, etc.

Enveloping learning opportunities for students into the cocoon of cutting-edge technologies changes students' interest levels, their engagement barometer, and their connectedness to lifelong learning. We need to seize this moment in time. It is imperative that we recognize and acknowledge the change that has been mandated as a condition of the summative assessments aligned to national and/or state standards. It is essential that we build on this stance positively so that our students can be prepared for college, their careers, and their present and future lives.

CHAPTER 6:
Communicating Effectively: Connecting Speaking and Listening with Reading and Writing Instruction

We wish for all of our students to advance through their lives as literate human beings. Being literate in the past meant being educated—defined as being able to read and write. Today, as individuals living in a global humanity, being literate has exploded to include so much more. Being literate necessitates thriving as an active, effective communicator, a savvy negotiator, an insightful problem-solver, a discerning viewer, and a flexible collaborator. Speaking and listening (oral language), as they weave the interplay with reading and writing (written language), have redefined literacy exponentially. They are core competencies vital for communication, success, and accomplishment in our world society. The skills I am proffering in this opening statement are easy to understand yet multidimensional and complex to master.

From the moment a child is born, all four elemental components of literacy are in play. They continue to be developed every day from birth on. By the time children enter school at the kindergarten level (age five), they have experienced 2.6 million minutes during which all four areas—listening, speaking, reading, and writing—have been exercised in different capacities. Between kindergarten and the end of eighth grade, students add on 4.2 million more minutes, with a hefty portion of that time spent learning in school, during which it is expected that students develop foundational skills, spiral those skills into proficiencies, and escalate the proficiencies into mastery, competence, and expertise.

The reason I provided the number of minutes in the scenario above is to bring attention to the amount of time children can be engaged in exciting and meaningful verbal interactions at home and at school. Think about how long one minute is when there is complete silence. If you can't conceptualize it, time it now. It is a vacuum—void of interaction or thought; it is a period of nothingness. One minute is a substantial expanse of time. Now, think about filling that same time frame with reading a great poem, listening to a page from a thrilling book, engaging with someone in a rich conversation, or asking detailed questions of an expert. Think about the interaction, enrichment, and learning that occur as students listen to learn and speak to communicate. As teachers, we need to enable students to productively engage with others, including student colleagues, so that their time is multiplied by great learning exchanges. Teachers should use every minute of precious class time to involve students in stimulating educational endeavors. Classroom conversation, dialogue, discussion, and debate are portrayals of a healthy, vibrant, and living learning community!

We practice getting better at communication throughout our lifetimes. As stated on the Skills You Need website (based on the research of Adler, Rosenfeld, and Proctor, 2001), "adults spend an average of 70 percent of their time engaged in some sort of communication; of this, an average of 45 percent is spent listening compared to 30 percent speaking, 16 percent reading, and 9 percent writing."

Given this information, it is critical to remember that reading, writing, speaking, and listening are skills that tread far beyond the reading program, the English language arts/literacy classroom, or the literacy teacher. These skills are rock-solidly embedded in every school learning experience in all subjects, at all grade levels. How well students absorb information by listening and how well they communicate that knowledge orally is a requisite skill in everything they are involved in on a daily basis.

It is important to note that all teachers, in essence, are teachers of all of these skill areas. Reading, writing, speaking, and listening need to be incorporated into content-based coursework with the goal that students become practiced at developing their acuity and proficiency geared to life success.

This chapter explores how speaking and listening will roll out in the scheme of the summative ELA assessments aligned to national and/or state standards. The chapter further looks at how conversation, productive talk, and critical listening lead to building skills in reading and writing and how speaking and listening serve as the foundation for reading and writing to occur seamlessly and habitually. Effective classroom practices are discussed in the chapter, which concludes with quality online sources for extending students' listening experiences.

Summative Assessments: What to Expect

Focus on Speaking and Listening

Based on the prominent assessment developers' informational releases as of this date, the thinking is that there will be assessments for speaking and listening available as a component of the commercially-available summative ELA assessments; however, they will be considered optional for the first several years. The goal is for speaking and listening to be measured, but this is also meant to be an authentic performance connected to daily classroom instruction. This conundrum has made the process of including the speaking and listening assessments as part of the initial administration of the assessments difficult. There is also a concern about the additional time the administration of the speaking and listening assessments would consume as part of the comprehensive assessment package. So giving states, districts, and schools the option to administer or not helps both the developers and districts better plan for the eventual implementation.

For those who give the speaking and listening assessments, prompts and rubrics will be available that classroom teachers can administer to assess students' performance. The students' performances will be locally scored and will not be included as part of the annual summative score on the summative assessment.

The summative ELA assessments will measure the speaking and listening communication skills students need for college and career readiness through two main types of experiences: extemporaneous speaking prompts and prepared/research speaking prompts.

The plan is for speaking and listening assessments to be built into the summative ELA assessments beginning in grade three and extending up through the higher grades. The time frame for the administration of the speaking and listening assessments is variable, given the districts' and schools' goals and scheduling.

At some grade levels, students will prepare for their speaking presentation by listening to a prerecorded reading, speech, media production, etc. They will then be given a prompt to which they will respond verbally, exhibiting good speaking skills. Students will interact with the audience and provide spontaneous oral responses by answering related questions and/or extending discussion topics, etc.

At other grade levels, students will be expected to do a bit of research on a topic given to them beforehand and prepare a formal presentation of the topic to their class. Students will present their topic and then engage with the audience to answer questions, extend their presentation, etc.

In most cases, teachers will score the presentations using a rubric provided by the assessment developers. The speaking and listening experiences will hinge upon their connection to reading and writing activities. This ensures rich classroom discussion and individualized speaking scenarios (debates, etc.) can be garnered from the content knowledge provided by the reading text passage and/or the written essay/response.

Focus on Listening to and Comprehending Content from Multimedia Sources

The design of the summative ELA assessments aligned to national and/or state standards embed listening skills directly into the reading and writing assessments students have been administered since Spring 2015.

Throughout the reading and writing components on both the performance and year-end summative ELA assessments, students will be interacting with text passages and text presented through multimedia formats. The multimedia formats include video clips, podcasts, recorded speeches, audio clips, etc. Students will need to listen carefully to the content being presented in these new formats, understand the information sufficiently, interpret or analyze the information adequately, and use the content effectively to provide the correct answers to the questions being asked and/or to support the extended written responses students are being asked to produce. This is a new challenge for students. The technology-based administration of the assessments supports the incorporation of the multimedia and digital content into the format and is a new way to present content information to students. In the past, with paper-based assessments this was not possible.

Therefore, it is important that focused daily instruction and classroom experiences incorporate this use of multimedia sources as sources of text. These experiences need to be supported throughout all of the content-based courses in which a student is enrolled.

The incorporation of multimedia sources into the assessments requires that headphones be provided to students as they take the assessment. This is a new addition to the assessment logistics that needs to be in place. In many cases, schools might need to purchase headphones for this purpose. However, the headphones can be used in classrooms as students interact with multimedia texts as content in their daily classroom work, projects, and assignments.

Effective Instruction: Speaking and Listening

Students need ample opportunities to engage in collaborative conversations in linguistically rich classrooms. They need to talk with teachers, share information with other students, discuss a passage from a book, think out loud as they solve a multistep problem, and negotiate with small groups over group decisions in project work. According to Wilkinson and Silliman (2000), "research indicates that both elementary and middle-grade readers' knowledge of oral-written language relationships are enriched when they talk informally with peers and more formally in student-dominated class discussions."

Even though speaking and listening are essential component areas of literacy instruction, other areas, particularly reading and writing, frequently receive primary attention, time allocation, and instructional focus. Robust speaking and listening skills are fundamental to students' success in both school and daily life and therefore merit equal importance. Thoughtful consideration needs to be given to the planning and implementation of a program of structured student learning objectives, activities, tasks, and assessments that embody the concept of classroom talk and collaborative conversations.

Teachers need to build students' abilities to engage in constructive conversations through practice. Speaking and listening instruction should be an integral component of daily lessons in each of the students' subject-area courses. Content-focused conversations in which students build upon each other's ideas as they interact with the subject material is the goal of the reading and writing standards we have discussed in prior chapters. Rich, academically-focused dialogue, discussion, and even debate, help students master the concepts of opinion development, critical thinking, and creating an evidence-based argument supported with factual knowledge.

In order to achieve these desired programmatic goals, students must have multiple opportunities to practice in classroom situations. Repeated practice will support students in developing an awareness of their oral language skills, improving their skills, and acquiring new skills as they participate in recurrent speaking and listening experiences. Having students participate in several key activities on a regular basis can help them demonstrate their understanding of complex information, ideas, and evidence presented orally. Conversely, through developing enhanced speaking skills, students can successfully present complex information, ideas, and evidence effectively through speech.

Face-to-face interaction is a skill that students must develop so that they can participate in a full life and challenge thinking. Using more complex language, negotiating strategically through logical thinking, and building a defined vocabulary enhances students' learning and propels them to higher levels of interaction, built on deep knowledge, powerful skills, and persuasive dispositions.

Classroom discussions, with partners and in small groups, help students communicate their thoughts appropriately. Students must be able to pay attention to the flow and content of conversations and actively take part in discussions, building off other students' ideas and thoughts. High-quality, structured classroom discussions focus all students on considering relevant information, assessing facts, making comparisons with other sources, developing their speaking points using evidence, and cementing their point of view on the topic.

Speaking/Listening in the Literacy Classroom

When thinking about speaking and listening in the literacy classroom, using shared reading as a strategy furthers these skills in the context of authentic reading and comprehension. Shared reading can be done as an entire class, in a small group, or with an individual student.

According to Button and Johnson (1997), "the shared reading experience offers a way teachers can use engaging texts and authentic literacy experiences to help children develop the strategies necessary for effective, independent reading" (p. 262). The Reading Rockets (2015) website states that "shared reading is an interactive reading experience that occurs when students join in or share the reading of a book or other text while guided and supported by a teacher."

Shared reading is an applicable strategy that can be employed at all grade levels. Allen (2000) supports this concept: "While it originates with young children, shared reading has potential through middle grades and high school."

According to the authors of the Common Core State Standards (2010), because "children's listening comprehension likely outpaces reading comprehension until the middle school years, it is particularly important that students in the earliest grades build knowledge through being read to as well as through reading, with the balance gradually shifting to reading independently. By reading a story or nonfiction selection aloud, teachers allow children to experience written language without the burden of decoding, granting them access to content that they may not be able to read and understand by themselves. Children are then free to focus their mental energy on the words and ideas presented in the text, and they will eventually be better prepared to tackle rich written content on their own" (Appendix A, p. 27).

However, the CCSS authors caution that "reading aloud to students in the upper grades should not, however, be used as a substitute for independent reading by students; read-alouds at this level should supplement and enrich what students are able to read by themselves" (Appendix A, p. 27).

Typically, students have a copy of the text in front of them, and they follow along in the text while observing and listening to the teacher or other reader model fluency and expression as he/she reads the selection, passage, or book out loud. Shared reading encourages students to join in the reading of the text. Shared reading is an effective way for students to enjoy the beauty of reading and improve their reading skills as well as their listening and speaking skills.

Speaking/Listening and the Common Core

Since the inception of standards implementation in the 1990s, many states developed and enacted standards for speaking and listening for students to align with their state standards for reading and writing. Many states even administered speaking and listening assessments along with their state assessment in reading and writing. The Common Core State Standards continue the tradition of connecting oral language with written language through the speaking and listening standards for all students in kindergarten through grade 12. In order for students to be prepared foundationally for college readiness and career/life success, students must participate in a sufficient variety of opportunities to take part in both spontaneous and structured conversations.

At each grade level, speaking and listening includes but is certainly not limited to class discussions, group work, and presentations. Interpersonal communication and collaboration are key aspects of mastering speaking and listening that students should be encouraged to develop. Having students develop critical friends, a circle of collaborators, and specific peer groups contributes to improving collaboration. A critical friend is "someone who is encouraging and supportive, but who also provides honest and often candid feedback that may be uncomfortable or difficult to hear. In short, a critical friend is someone who agrees to speak truthfully, but constructively, about weaknesses, problems, and emotionally charged issues" (The Glossary of Education Reform, 2013).

Rich dialogues must be conducted in a number of varying configurations—partner groups (two students), small groups, and whole class. "For students to actively participate in these situations, they must be able to contribute accurate, relevant information; respond to and develop what others have said; make comparisons and contrasts; and analyze and synthesize a multitude of ideas in various domains" (Common Core State Standards—ELA/Literacy, p. 22).

The six standards listed below each have grade-level indicators that are expected to be mastered.

CCSS College and Career Readiness Anchor Standards for Speaking and Listening	
Source: Common Core State Standards (2010)	
Comprehension and Collaboration	
CCR 1	Prepare for and participate effectively in a range of conversations and collaborations with diverse partners, building on others' ideas and expressing their own clearly and persuasively.
CCR 2	Integrate and evaluate information presented in diverse media and formats, including visually, quantitatively, and orally.
CCR 3	Evaluate a speaker's point of view, reasoning, and use of evidence and rhetoric.
Presentation of Knowledge and Ideas	
CCR 4	Present information, findings, and supporting evidence such that listeners can follow the line of reasoning and the organization, development, and style are appropriate to task, purpose, and audience.
CCR 5	Make strategic use of digital media and visual displays of data to express information and enhance understanding of presentations.
CCR 6	Adapt speech to a variety of contexts and communicative tasks, demonstrating command of formal English when indicated or appropriate.

Here is an overview of the speaking and listening skills needing mastery at the eighth-grade level:

CCSS Speaking and Listening Standards: Grade 8
Source: Common Core State Standards (2010)
Comprehension and Collaboration
CCSS.ELA-Literacy.SL.8.1: Engage effectively in a range of collaborative discussions (one-on-one, in groups, and teacher led) with diverse partners on grade 8 topics, texts, and issues, building on others' ideas and expressing their own clearly. a. Come to discussions prepared, having read or researched material under study; explicitly draw on that preparation by referring to evidence on the topic, text, or issue to probe and reflect on ideas under discussion. b. Follow rules for collegial discussions and decision-making, track progress toward specific goals and deadlines, and define individual roles as needed. c. Pose questions that connect the ideas of several speakers and respond to others' questions and comments with relevant evidence, observations, and ideas. d. Acknowledge new information expressed by others, and, when warranted, qualify or justify their own views in light of the evidence presented.
CCSS.ELA-Literacy.SL.8.2: Analyze the purpose of information presented in diverse media and formats (e.g., visually, quantitatively, orally) and evaluate the motives (e.g., social, commercial, political) behind its presentation.
CCSS.ELA-Literacy.SL.8.3: Delineate a speaker's argument and specific claims, evaluating the soundness of the reasoning and relevance and sufficiency of the evidence and identifying when irrelevant evidence is introduced.
Presentation of Knowledge and Ideas
CCSS.ELA-Literacy.SL.8.4: Present claims and findings, emphasizing salient points in a focused, coherent manner with relevant evidence, sound valid reasoning, and well-chosen details; use appropriate eye contact, adequate volume, and clear pronunciation.
CCSS.ELA-Literacy.SL.8.5: Integrate multimedia and visual displays into presentations to clarify information, strengthen claims and evidence, and add interest.
CCSS.ELA-Literacy.SL.8.6: Adapt speech to a variety of contexts and tasks, demonstrating command of formal English when indicated or appropriate. (See grade 8 Language standards 1 and 3 for specific expectations.)

As you can see, there are intricate connections between speaking and listening. The standards represent both areas. They constantly overlap one another, and inter-relationships between speaking and listening, between reading and writing, and between oral and written language mean that no one strand should be considered on its own. Vocabulary is important to all four areas as well.

The standards require students to have two levels of active engagement. One area is on communication/collaboration and the second area is on presentation. Either is incomplete without the other. Students, having communicated orally in discussions, posing questions, justifying the factual information and/or point of view, etc. must also be able to present information in a formal manner. They must utilize oral proficiency backed up with evidence-based claims in an organized fashion. Their presentations should be delivered with presence and confidence and reinforced with visual representations (and sometimes written documentation) that support their position.

The modes of presentation are both traditional and steeped in digital technologies and commingled, as applicable, to deliver the finest product that represents deep understanding, superior organization, salient points accompanied by comprehensible evidence, and conclusions drawn from inferences with proposed solutions that are viable.

The Classroom:
10 Practical Strategies on
Enhancing Speaking and Listening

1. Create a question-centered classroom. As adults, finding solutions and solving problems is accompanied by posing salient and probing questions to further knowledge, extracting data, gleaning insight, and getting to the core of the issue. Students should be afforded the same experiences. A question-centered classroom promotes speaking and listening as the core classroom focus. This inquiry-based methodology sets the stage for students to identify problem-based scenarios and research issues and questions to develop their knowledge or solutions through discovery. According to Wilson (2015), "encouraging children to think, to learn, to remember, to make inferences and connections through questions is a very ancient form of education—one that needs to be perpetuated, understood, and practiced."

The first step is to add one question to all of your classroom interactions and discussions with students. The question is "why?" Students must develop an inquisitive nature and curiosity. The word is at the core of inquiry and investigation. A question-centered classroom also structures questions from the taxonomy perspective, in which students experience questions of various kinds leading up to high-level questions. "A question-centered classroom includes question-posing, exploring, negotiating, clarifying, extending, seeking, answering, all leading to more questions as students engage in authentic literacy activities—authentic work that is integrated, not practicing skills in isolation" (Routman, 2000, p. 13).

2. Model good speaking and listening performance for students. Teachers are the best models for the performance behaviors that they wish students to emulate. Teachers need to carry out good listening skills, including facing and maintaining eye contact with the listeners, focusing full attention on the speaker without interrupting him or her, paraphrasing points to avoid misunderstanding the speaker's thoughts, and responding appropriately to show understanding.

When practicing effective speaking skills, teachers must exude confidence and poise, use correct grammar and structure, and utilize sophisticated vocabulary. They must also connect with the audience through appropriate storytelling, paraphrase the other person's ideas before responding, vary tone and pace, and punctuate words with complementary gestures. Throughout the course of their instruction, teachers should vary their mode of oral presentation to meet the goals of the experience. For example, if a teacher is reading a poem that is rhythmic in nature, the teacher's voice and rhythm should match the poem. Similarly, if the reading is of a famous speech, the tone should replicate the original or similar intonation, expression, and style of the speaker.

Providing students with exemplary modeling, as well as high-quality speaking and listening interactions, promotes their skill development and increases students' fluency and proficiency in incorporating the modeled strategies seamlessly into their own repertoire.

3. Teach active listening techniques to students. One way to improve listening skills is to practice active listening. According to Heberle (2015), "active listening goes beyond just listening. Active listening means being attentive to what someone else is saying. The goal of active listening is to understand the feelings and views of the person."

Students should be taught to listen for the big ideas when someone is speaking—not just the words they are saying. The idea is to get the entire picture, not just disconnected or isolated pieces. Students need to pay attention.

Linking together bits of information to uncover the ideas and thoughts of others is not an easy skill. This takes practice and paying very close attention to the speaker. Students need to paraphrase and summarize.

It also involves letting the speaker know that you are listening to what he or she is saying through gesturing, nodding, and using body language (sitting forward in your seat). Students need to provide this feedback to speakers.

Active listening is important in effective communication, and students will continue to use the skills in future school experiences, at home, in social interactions, and in future career opportunities.

4. Schedule book talks. Organizing scheduled book talks gives students opportunities to speak favorably about books they have read through a structured conversation or presentation to their classmates. Book talks often include reading from the book itself, which promotes reading practice. When preparing for the book talk, students will have rehearsed their presentation and practiced the segment of the book that they intend to share. Because the book talk gives students the opportunity to role-play "being an expert" and they provide compelling reasons for others to read the same book, audience members often seize the recommendation and read the same book or books by the same author.

Some general guidelines for preparing students to conduct book talks include the following steps.

Book Talks—Steps to Consider	
Guiding Steps	**Helpful Hints**
Begin with an introduction.	Students should be encouraged to make this interesting so that it garners the attention of the audience.
Give the title of the book and the name of the author.	Students should practice the proper pronunciation of names.
Provide background information on the author.	Include other books he/she has written. Check for information on the book cover or introductory pages.
Let the audience know the genre.	Examples include: fantasy, myth, mystery, science fiction, biography, etc.
Tell the audience about the setting.	Where and when did the story take place?
Identify and describe the main character(s) in your book.	Don't just list the characters. Introduce them to the audience and help them get to know the characters.
Explain the main conflict or struggle that the character had to deal with or overcome.	Explain why this was the conflict.

-continued

Book Talks—Steps to Consider	
Guiding Steps	**Helpful Hints**
Tell the audience about the plot of the story.	Be brief. Share some interesting details, but don't say too much that you give away the whole story!
Capture the mood of this book.	Is the book thrilling, funny, sad, scary?
Convey the theme.	What is the author really trying to tell us? Look for the central idea or lesson about life that the author wants us to know.
Explain why you selected your passage—usually no longer that one short page.	Read a passage that is interesting or enlightening. It could be an interesting quotation, a good description, or a memorable line or paragraph.
Report your overall rating of the book.	How much did you like the book? Why or why not? Give some details.
Who would you recommend this book to and why? Tell why the audience should want to go out and get this book.	What do you remember most about the book?

5. Apply the think-pair-share strategy. The think-pair-share strategy was originally created in 1982 (Lyman), but it seems that it has been with educators forever.

Think-pair-share is a structured technique designed to differentiate instruction by assigning time for students to think about a topic or problem. This independent thinking time motivates students to compose their personal thoughts and share their views and ideas with a peer. Using this strategy encourages student participation at several levels and involves both the individual student and students working together in pairs. This strategy is applicable across all class sizes and grade levels and doubles student engagement time instantly.

Students follow three well-defined steps (Allen Simon, 2015):

- Think—Teachers initiate the process by asking a specific higher-level question about the text or topic students will be discussing. Students think independently about the question that has been posed, consider what they know, and form ideas of their own (one to three minutes).

- Pair—Students are grouped in pairs (by teacher designation or student self-selection) to discuss their thoughts. Students articulate their ideas with their partner. Students consider the other's thoughts by asking questions of their partner (two to five minutes).

- Share—Student pairs share their ideas when the teacher expands the conversation into whole-class discussion. Often, students are more comfortable presenting ideas to a group with the support of a partner. In addition, students' ideas have become more refined through this three-step process.

Discussion questions, partner reading, topic development, and action plan formulation can be conducted via this clear-cut strategy. Think-pair-share helps students develop conceptual understanding of a topic, the ability to filter information and draw conclusions, and the capacity to consider other points of view.

6. Conduct talk show interviews. This format should be very familiar to students. In the media today, there are examples of quality talk show segments during which prominent politicians, entertainers, and everyday people are interviewed by a host or a panel of hosts. Based on the grade-level curriculum, particularly focusing on the content areas of English language arts/literacy, science, social studies, health, and the arts, there are many opportunities to find topics of conflict, controversies, for/against positions, and differences of opinion. Modeling the structured conversation that occurs in a talk show interview, students can perform the various roles: interviewer, interviewee, expert, and audience member. The students participating as part of the interview have a primary role to share information correctly and accurately, provide evidence to align with their position, offer opinions, and build rapport with the audience members. The students who are audience members are also active participants as they are key listeners. Audience members get to ask clarifying questions, prod the speakers to elaborate on their speaking points, give a differing opinion or point of view, offer suggestions for solutions, and provide feedback.

These talk show interviews can be conducted as an introductory activity to a new unit and also as a culminating activity. The format can also be expanded beyond the classroom to a scenario in which the class conducting the talk show performs it for a larger audience. Perhaps the class presents themselves as part of a grade-level activity, and other classes attend their talk show as part of the audience. These talk shows can be hosted periodically and can also deal with local, neighborhood, and school issues.

Lastly, in order to better replicate real life and to infuse technology skills into the process, the talk show could be recorded by students. The goal of taping the episode is twofold:

- The students and the class could watch their performance as it is played back. They could watch it a number of times for a number of different purposes. Overall, students would take on the role of "reviewers" and analyze and assess their own and others' performances. Their comments would give insight and reflection to improve their practices for future sessions.
- The taped version could be televised, streamed, etc. over school-wide, closed networks and public-access cable channels so that students could view their productions as essential to their school community and local community. Proper student media releases would need to be secured and other school district protocols would need to be followed.

7. Go to four corners. Use all four corners of the classroom to get students moving in this revealing activity. Write the following opinion words on four large pieces of paper: Strongly Agree, Somewhat Agree, Strongly Disagree, and Somewhat Disagree. Place a sign in each corner of the classroom.

Pose different topics to the class. Choose topics based on the students' age group. Gravitate toward topics that are issue oriented and controversial. For example: Schools should eliminate sports teams; there should be boys-only and girls-only schools; or schools should eliminate homework. Once the topic is chosen, write the topic on the board.

Students will be instructed by the teacher to move to the corner of the room that best describes their opinion (how they feel) about the topic. The groups are given a few minutes to discuss the topic and write down the reasons for their decisions. Students work in their groups to verbalize their positions; each corner has five minutes to discuss the problem and firm up the key points the group wishes to emphasize.

Each group selects a spokesperson to articulate the group's stance. The spokesperson has 30 seconds to summarize the group's thoughts and influence the other groups, swaying their positions. All of the groups must listen intently while other groups present their arguments.

After the first corner presents, any students who have been persuaded through the group's convincing arguments move to that appropriate corner. In turn, each group will be directed to present their group's position. Students should continue to move to the appropriate corners if they have changed their minds.

The outcome of this activity is that students will be able to express their positions, as well as opposing arguments, on a particular issue.

8. Play "For and Against." Students need to think—and think quickly on their feet—for this activity. Students must be prepared to speak about both sides of a pertinent topic, controversial issue, or pending problem. What do students really think? Through this structured activity, students will be required to speak from the "for" and "against" positions on a hot topic, divisive matter, or critical concern and articulate their thoughts to their classmates. There are various ways of conducting this type of activity. Students can be given the topic by the teacher, or they can self-select a topic of interest to them. They are not given any time to think about it beforehand. This is an on-demand speaking activity.

Once given the topic, the student must speak "for" the topic for 30 seconds. A timer is set for 30 seconds. When the timer beeps, the same student then speaks "against" the topic for the next 30 seconds. The activity continues with the same student speaking again "for" the topic for 30 more seconds. Once more, the student speaks "against" the topic for the next 30 seconds. The teacher can determine how many rounds of speaking a single student will engage in. This can be determined by the students' grade level, proficiency level, or resilience. The number of rounds can be increased as students partake in it over the course of the school year. Additionally, this activity can be modified to include a substantive number of students, or even an entire class. The teacher would need to set a specific number of rounds per student or have students listen to a partner and then reverse roles.

This speaking activity promotes quick thinking, thinking about the topic at hand, and speaking on both positions of the topic. Students should be encouraged to use evidence and data when they present both views on the subject. They should provide their best compelling argument as they verbally discuss this topic with their classmates. This activity can also easily be conducted in partner pairs and small groups.

9. Role-play stakeholders' positions. Role-playing is an effective way to get students interested in literature, social studies, science, and the arts. It can facilitate their engagement with and learning of content-based material in an authentic mode. Role-playing can include memorization of the text or reading the text aloud as the students play their roles. There are also opportunities to extend learning and foster creative thinking by having students project what happens next. What is the sequel to the story? By applying knowledge gained from role-playing and original ideas, students can generate creative and novel solutions and scenarios. According to Blatner (2009), role-playing is the best way to develop the skills of initiative, communication, problem-solving, self-awareness, and working cooperatively in teams.

Students can role-play by investigating debatable situations in which there are a variety of stakeholders involved. Students first make a list of stakeholders involved in the scenario. One such sample topic is the mayor wishing to close the local library on weekends. The stakeholder groups may include students, parents, teachers, taxpayers, library employees, and senior citizens. Each student would be assigned to a stakeholder group of several students (depending on the size of the class).

Each group takes a positional stand and creates an argument for or against the situation, based on the stakeholder they represent. Students prepare individually and collaboratively with their groups. Groups then present their arguments to the class. After each group presentation, the other stakeholder groups ask questions about its stance.

10. Stage mock trials. Mock trials impart valuable learning for students at all grade levels. They are an activity that can be coupled with the curriculum or units of study across multiple subjects.

The process of mock trials helps students understand the legal system, practice critical thinking, and gain confidence with public speaking by assuming the roles of attorneys and witnesses in a fictional criminal or civil trial. Individuals, such as a character from a fictional novel, a historical figure, a scientist, a politician, or a performer (musician, comedian) could all be put on trial and accused of a relevant "crime"—blamed for a negative incident, conflict, or outcome.

Students get firsthand, authentic experience dealing with the complexity of the challenges that judges, lawyers, and juries face in determining which facts are relevant and important and what legal arguments are effective. Students partake in roles on both the prosecution side and the defense side of the debate. This kind of activity needs to be planned and prepared in advance with different members of the class being allotted different roles (e.g., the accused, the lawyers, the witnesses, the judge, and court staff) so that they can research and practice arguing the sides and ask significant questions.

Students who are not given specific roles become members of the jury who will decide the fate of the figure on trial.

Online Resources for Extending Learning

There are numerous online sites that provide speech banks containing a wealth of text, audio, and video speeches and other offerings that can broaden the repertoire of resources included in teachers' lessons, student projects, literacy experiences, and content-based offerings.

- American Rhetoric—Online speech bank with a database of and an index to 5,000-plus full-text, audio, and video versions of public speeches, sermons, legal proceedings, lectures, debates, interviews, and other recorded media events.
- Internet Archive—Great platform to remember important moments in time. Speeches include farewell addresses, abdication addresses, election eve campaign speeches, and presidential campaign addresses.

- The Guardian's Great Interviews of the 20th Century and Great Speeches of the 20th Century—Transcripts and archival materials accompany the pieces.

- The History Channel—Features famous historical speeches as video clips and audio clips.

- LibriVox—Extensive collection of free audio books read by volunteers; the goal is to record every book in the public domain.

- Oyez: U.S. Supreme Court Media—Multimedia archive devoted to the Supreme Court of the United States and its work. Provides authoritative information on all justices and offers a virtual reality of portions of the Supreme Court building, including the chambers of some of the justices.

- Project Gutenberg: The Audio Books Project—Audio books in a number of languages. Classics include Aesop's Fables and works by Jane Austen, Hans Christian Andersen, and Lewis Carroll.

- StoryCorps—More than 45,000 interviews by everyday people have been archived. Series of animated audiovisual recordings that students will enjoy are part of the site. There are also resources for coaching students to conduct effective interviews.

- TED—Brief talks by experts who speak about their area or interest. There are TED talks on a wide variety of topics. Age-appropriate talks for students can be located by searching for "talks for kids."

Summative Assessments: Sample Items Under Development

Speaking and listening is not anticipated to be part of the initial administration of the summative ELA assessments aligned to national and/or state standards. Resources are currently under development. Without having any concrete samples that are research based and vetted by the assessment developers for their alignment to the summative ELA assessments, close attention will help us monitor and become astutely aware of future developments. As the new tasks materialize, we will expand and adjust our practices in a timely fashion to include elements of the models put forth.

In the meantime, for many students, their speaking and listening skills are far more sophisticated than their reading and/or writing skills. Educators must be purposeful and seize the opportunity to have speaking and listening be the impetus and the connective tissue with reading and writing goals and activities. Teachers should continue to be proactive in creating vigorous opportunities for students to carry out authentic learning activities that encourage student talk and collaborative conversations aligned to engaging literacy lessons.

Summary

Chapter 6 is the final chapter of this book. This chapter focused on speaking and listening as the glue that bonds literacy together for all students and makes English language arts/literacy come alive. Considering these skills as the overarching component of effective literacy maximizes their importance. Speaking and listening can be leveraged as the gateway to integrating literacy learning for students. It is for the readers to think about how these two skill areas are so effortlessly part of our being that we often take them for granted. They are often thought of so differently from the other component parts of effective literacy instruction.

We really don't ever think of speaking and listening as a school subject the way we do reading and writing. Most students don't get grades in speaking and listening. Throughout my career, I have yet to ever hear of a student who passed or failed speaking and listening. All students successfully develop these skills continuously throughout their lifetimes, and the skills are enhanced through experiential learning based in communication.

Leveraging the power of speaking and listening to serve as the impetus to strengthen and enhance students' literacy skills in reading and writing seems like a natural fit, and we need to strategically utilize these areas to transform students into the most prolific readers and writers they can be. Use speaking and listening as the vehicle to have students engage with complex text, use high-level vocabulary words, discuss what they have read, and take a positional stand and defend it in writing based on what they may have initially produced as an oral argument—all viable and worthy goals to strive for as instructional leaders in classrooms and in schools.

Final Reflections

As the narrative of this book comes to a close, much information has been written, many experts quoted, and a multitude of suggestions, ideas, techniques, and examples have been offered. The purpose of this book is to guide practice that will foster a causal relationship between the rich literacy best practices that occur in classrooms daily and student success and high-level performance on any given summative ELA assessment aligned to national and/or state standards.

Student learning and the transfer of skills with the application of knowledge in new situations is the driving goal. I maintain the belief that great teaching and great learning will proactively cause success on the summative assessments. For far too long, educators have been reactive to the data and results of state summative assessments. We must be proactive from this moment forward.

The trajectory of new standards has been set out before us. In most cases, once a new set of standards are adopted, they are periodically reviewed and adjusted to best meet the needs of states and their districts. The present standards have been adopted at different time frames over the past five years in most states. Therefore, as time continues over the next few years, student learning outcomes from the implementation of the standards and data resulting from the summative assessments aligned to the standards will be reviewed and appraised. Potential adjustments to the standards may be made to fine-tune their influence and impact on student learning. The standards, both national and state level, are the base level, foundational elements upon which curriculum, instruction, assessment, professional learning, parental support, and community collaboration are designed, developed, implemented, and assessed. We stand at the right moment in time to begin to work toward these new goals. We should not underestimate our students or ourselves to do this work well. We must do it. We must work together. A cycle of collaborative, continuous improvement must be embraced. The students themselves should be the ones demanding that we demonstrate how they can do better and what they have to do to achieve high levels of success in elementary grades, middle school, and high school. We must remember that the ultimate purpose of our educational efforts is student learning.

Concepts that have been researched for this book and written about in the preceding chapters have been written about through history in different and unique ways. Having students become prolific readers and writers has been an established goal since ancient times. However, we are living in a most modern century, and all of our students are entitled to an education that will keep them moving forward exponentially. Consider that a population of our present students will live productive lives into the beginning of the next century! They will need to continue to grow daily in their knowledge and skills to live in a very different world. Literacy in reading, writing, speaking, and listening are vital skills that will continue to be paramount to their successful futures.

As professional educators, we are expected to possess the knowledge, skills, and dispositions to accomplish what is expected of the Common Core State Standards and on the summative assessments aligned with national and/or state standards. However, how we are presently engaging in the work needs to be thoughtfully transformed into what works best for students—all of the students. At this time, too many of our students are not experiencing success in school. The power and potential of this journey is to carry out the work so that every single student strives for excellence and succeeds at the highest levels.

Like the performance of a symphony orchestra, success in literacy comes from practice over long periods of time. When all the parts come together, it is a beautiful performance.

Start somewhere. Start now. Learn to choose the best complex texts and strategically use close reading to involve students. Work to enhance your present writing plan to focus on opinion/argument construction and writing. Pledge to construct text-dependent questions for student assignments and commit to asking text-dependent questions during discussions, reflective readings, etc. Think about designing speaking and listening performance tasks for unit plans. Use technology to pursue innovative iterations of research-based assignments and tasks. Begin to work toward a new reality in your classroom of ensuring that all students can work smarter, achieve more, and do things they didn't even suspect would make them better students, better adults, and better human beings.

I wish you much professional success and personal fulfillment in your professional learning and in your work with students to accomplish the academic goals set forth in national and state standards and the summative ELA assessments aligned to those standards. I trust that this book, *From the Classroom to the Test* provides inspiration and information to guide your future efforts.

Summative ELA Assessments: Sample Items

This section provides examples of summative assessment items. These samples are provided to showcase possible formats and tasks to support teachers' work as they coach students in demonstrating the skills and understandings critical for success on these assessments but, most importantly, in future college, career, and life settings. Please note: The passages and questions included are from outside sources as indicated in each section and in the references for this book. An answer key is included on pages 203–207.

Grade 3 Sample Items

You will read four parts of the story "The Fisherman and His Wife" by Jacob and Wilhelm Grimm. After each part of the story, called a scene, you will then answer questions about the story.

"The Fisherman and His Wife"

by Jacob and Wilhelm Grimm, translated by Lucy Crane

SCENE 1:

1   There was once a fisherman and his wife who lived together in a hovel by the sea-shore, and the fisherman went out every day with his hook and line to catch fish, and he angled and angled.

2   One day he was sitting with his rod and looking into the clear water, and he sat and sat. At last down went the line to the bottom of the water, and when he drew it up he found a great flounder on the hook.

3   And the flounder said to him, "Fisherman, listen to me; let me go, I am not a real fish but an enchanted prince. What good shall I be to you if you land me? I shall not taste well; so put me back into the water again, and let me swim away."

4   "Well," said the fisherman, "no need of so many words about the matter; as you can speak, I had much rather let you swim away." Then he put him back into the clear water, and the flounder sank to the bottom... Then the fisherman got up and went home to his wife in their hovel.

5   "Well, husband," said the wife, "have you caught nothing to-day?"

6   "No," said the man—"that is, I did catch a flounder, but as he said he was an enchanted prince, I let him go again."

7   "Then, did you wish for nothing?" said the wife.

8   "No," said the man; "what should I wish for?"

Grade 3 passages and questions with responses for "The Fisherman and His Wife" by Jacob and Wilhelm Grimm, translated by Lucy Crane, reprinted with permission from Student Achievement Partners (2015).

9   "Oh dear!" said the wife; "and it is so dreadful always to live in this evil-smelling hovel; you might as well have wished for a little cottage; go again and call him; tell him we want a little cottage, I daresay he will give it us; go, and be quick."

10 And when he went back, the sea was green and yellow, and not nearly so clear. So he stood and said,

> "O man, O man!—if man you be,
> Or flounder, flounder, in the sea—
> Such a tiresome wife I've got,
> For she wants what I do not."

11 Then the flounder came swimming up, and said, "Now then, what does she want?"

12 "Oh," said the man, "you know when I caught you my wife says I ought to have wished for something. She does not want to live any longer in the hovel, and would rather have a cottage.

13 "Go home with you," said the flounder, "she has it already."

14 So the man went home, and found, instead of the hovel, a little cottage, and his wife was sitting on a bench before the door. And she took him by the hand, and said to him,

15 "Come in and see if this is not a great improvement."

16 So they went in, and there was a little house-place and a beautiful little bedroom, a kitchen and larder, with all sorts of furniture, and iron and brassware of the very best. And at the back was a little yard with fowls and ducks, and a little garden full of green vegetables and fruit.

17 "Look," said the wife, "is not that nice?"

18 "Yes," said the man, "if this can only last we shall be very well contented."

19 "We will see about that," said the wife. And after a meal they went to bed.

Grade 3 passages and questions with responses for "The Fisherman and His Wife" by Jacob and Wilhelm Grimm, translated by Lucy Crane, reprinted with permission from Student Achievement Partners (2015).

Question 1

The following question has two parts. Answer Part A and then answer Part B.

Part A

What does the word "dreadful" mean in paragraph 9 of Scene 1?

A. sad
B. scary
C. horrible
D. embarrassing

Part B

Which words from paragraph 9 of Scene 1 best help the reader understand the meaning of "dreadful"?

A. "Oh dear!"
B. "evil-smelling"
C. "little cottage"
D. "go, and be quick."

Grade 3 passages and questions with responses for "The Fisherman and His Wife" by Jacob and Wilhelm Grimm, translated by Lucy Crane, reprinted with permission from Student Achievement Partners (2015).

Question 2

What does the fisherman mean when he uses the word "contented" in paragraph 18?

A. They should be happy.
B. They will be rich.
C. They will be famous
D. They should be honored.

Question 3

The following question has two parts. Answer Part A and then answer Part B.

Part A

Which word best describes the fisherman in Scene 1?

A. Greedy
B. Unwise
C. Curious
D. Kind

Part B

What action from the story best supports the answer to Part A?

A. He goes fishing every day.
B. He releases the fish back into the water.
C. He tells his wife about the enchanted fish he caught.
D. He tells the fish that his wife wants a better house to live in.

Grade 3 passages and questions with responses for "The Fisherman and His Wife" by
Jacob and Wilhelm Grimm, translated by Lucy Crane, reprinted with permission from
Student Achievement Partners (2015).

SCENE 2:

20 So all went well for a week or fortnight, when the wife said,

21 "Look here, husband, the cottage is really too confined, and the yard and garden are so small. I think the flounder had better get us a larger house. I should like very much to live in a large stone castle; so go to your fish and he will send us a castle."

22 "O my dear wife," said the man, "the cottage is good enough; what do we want a castle for?"

23 "We want one," said the wife; "go along with you; the flounder can give us one."

24 "Now, wife," said the man, "the flounder gave us the cottage; I do not like to go to him again, he may be angry."

25 "Go along," said the wife, "he might just as well give us it as not; do as I say!"

26 The man felt very reluctant and unwilling; and he said to himself, "It is not the right thing to do;" nevertheless he went.

27 So when he came to the seaside, the water was purple and dark blue and grey and thick, and not green and yellow as before. And he stood and said,

> "O man, O man!—if man you be,
> Or flounder, flounder, in the sea—
> Such a tiresome wife I've got,
> For she wants what I do not."

28 "Now then, what does she want?" said the flounder.

29 "Oh," said the man, half frightened, "she wants to live in a large stone castle."

Grade 3 passages and questions with responses for "The Fisherman and His Wife" by Jacob and Wilhelm Grimm, translated by Lucy Crane, reprinted with permission from Student Achievement Partners (2015).

30 "Go home with you, she is already standing before the door,"
said the flounder.

31 Then the man went home, as he supposed, but when he got there, there
stood in the place of the cottage a great castle of stone, and his wife was
standing on the steps, about to go in; so she took him by the hand, and said,
"Let us enter."

32 With that he went in with her, and in the castle was a great hall with a
marble pavement, and there were a great many servants, who led them
through large doors, and the passages were decked with tapestry, and the
rooms with golden chairs and tables, and crystal chandeliers hanging from
the ceiling; and all the rooms had carpets. And the tables were covered with
eatables…for anyone who wanted them. And at the back of the house was a
great stable-yard for horses and cattle, and carriages of the finest; besides,
there was a splendid large garden, with the most beautiful flowers and fine
fruit trees, and a pleasance[1] full half a mile long, with deer and oxen and
sheep, and everything that heart could wish for.

33 "There!" said the wife, "is not this beautiful?"

34 "Oh yes," said the man, "if it will only last we can live in this fine castle
and be very well contented."

35 "We will see about that," said the wife, "in the meanwhile we will sleep
upon it." With that they went to bed.

[1] A quiet, tree-planted area with paths

Grade 3 passages and questions with responses for "The Fisherman and His Wife" by
Jacob and Wilhelm Grimm, translated by Lucy Crane, reprinted with permission from
Student Achievement Partners (2015).

145

Question 4

The following question has two parts. Answer Part A and then answer Part B.

Part A

In paragraph 26 of Scene 2, why does the husband say that asking the fish for a castle "is not the right thing to do"?

A. He loves the little cottage the fish gave him.
B. He does not want a larger place to take care of.
C. He feels his wife is asking for too much from the fish.
D. He believes there are more important things to wish for.

Part B

How does the husband think the fish will respond?

A. He thinks the fish will become angry with him.
B. He thinks the fish will ignore him when he calls it from the sea.
C. He thinks the fish will tell him he is being selfish with his wishes.
D. He thinks the fish will ask him for a favor in return.

Grade 3 passages and questions with responses for "The Fisherman and His Wife" by Jacob and Wilhelm Grimm, translated by Lucy Crane, reprinted with permission from Student Achievement Partners (2015).

Question 5

The following question has two parts. Answer Part A and then answer Part B.

Part A

How does Scene 2 of the story build on Scene 1?

A. Scene 1 shows that the wife is thankful for her husband, and Scene 2 allows the reader to see that the husband is thankful for his wife.
B. Scene 1 shows the wife is unhappy with her home, and Scene 2 allows the reader to see that the wife wants more than she needs.
C. Scene 1 shows that the husband does not believe the fish is enchanted, and Scene 2 provides proof that it is.
D. Scene 1 shows that the wife is greedy, and Scene 2 shows that the husband becomes greedy as well.

Part B

Which sentence from Scene 2 supports the answer to Part A?

A. "'I think the flounder had better get us a larger house.'"
B. "'Go home with you, she is already standing before the door,' said the flounder."
C. "'There!' said the wife, 'is not this beautiful?'"
D. "'Oh yes,' said the man, 'if it will only last we can live in this fine castle and be very well contented.'"

Grade 3 passages and questions with responses for "The Fisherman and His Wife" by Jacob and Wilhelm Grimm, translated by Lucy Crane, reprinted with permission from Student Achievement Partners (2015).

SCENE 3:

36 The next morning the wife was awake first, just at the break of day, and she looked out and saw from her bed the beautiful country lying all round. The man took no notice of it, so she poked him in the side with her elbow, and said,

37 "Husband, get up and just look out of the window. Look, just think if we could be king over all this country. Just go to your fish and tell him we should like to be king."

38 "Now, wife," said the man, "what should we be kings for? I don't want to be king."

39 "Well," said the wife, "if you don't want to be king, I will be king."

40 "Now, wife," said the man, "what do you want to be king for? I could not ask him such a thing."

41 "Why not?" said the wife, "you must go directly all the same; I must be king."

42 So the man went, very much put out that his wife should want to be king.

43 "It is not the right thing to do—not at all the right thing," thought the man. He did not at all want to go, and yet he went all the same.

44 And when he came to the sea the water was quite dark grey, and rushed far inland, and had an ill smell. And he stood and said,

> "O man, O man!—if man you be,
> Or flounder, flounder, in the sea—
> Such a tiresome wife I've got,
> For she wants what I do not."

45 "Now then, what does she want?" said the fish.

46 "Oh dear!" said the man, "she wants to be king."

47 "Go home with you, she is so already," said the fish.

Grade 3 passages and questions with responses for "The Fisherman and His Wife" by Jacob and Wilhelm Grimm, translated by Lucy Crane, reprinted with permission from Student Achievement Partners (2015).

48 So the man went back, and as he came to the palace he saw it was very much larger, and had great towers and splendid gateways; the herald stood before the door, and a number of soldiers with kettle-drums and trumpets. And when he came inside everything was of marble and gold, and there were many curtains with great golden tassels. Then he went through the doors of the salon to where the great throne-room was, and there was his wife sitting upon a throne of gold and diamonds, and she had a great golden crown on, and the sceptre[2] in her hand was of pure gold and jewels, and on each side stood six pages[3] in a row, each one a head shorter than the other. So the man went up to her and said,

49 "Well, wife, so now you are king!"

50 "Yes," said the wife, "now I am king."

51 So then he stood and looked at her, and when he had gazed at her for some time he said,

52 "Well, wife, this is fine for you to be king! Now there is nothing more to wish for."

53 "O husband!" said the wife, seeming quite restless, "I am tired of this already. Go to your fish and tell him that now I am king I must be emperor."

54 "Now, wife," said the man, "what do you want to be emperor for?"

55 "Husband," said she, "go and tell the fish I want to be emperor."

56 "Oh dear!" said the man, "he could not do it—I cannot ask him such a thing. There is but one emperor at a time; the fish can't possibly make any one emperor—indeed he can't."

57 "Now, look here," said the wife, "I am king, and you are only my husband, so will you go at once? Go along! For if he was able to make me king he is able to make me emperor; and I will and must be emperor, so go along!"

58 So he was obliged to go; and as he went he felt very uncomfortable about it, and he thought to himself, "It is not at all the right thing to do; to want to be emperor is really going too far; the flounder will soon be beginning to get tired of this."

[2] A staff used during ceremonies to show importance

[3] Young boys who run errands

Grade 3 passages and questions with responses for "The Fisherman and His Wife" by Jacob and Wilhelm Grimm, translated by Lucy Crane, reprinted with permission from Student Achievement Partners (2015).

Question 6

In Scenes 1, 2, and 3, the wife asks for a different house. To complete the chart below, use the details from the list to describe each house.

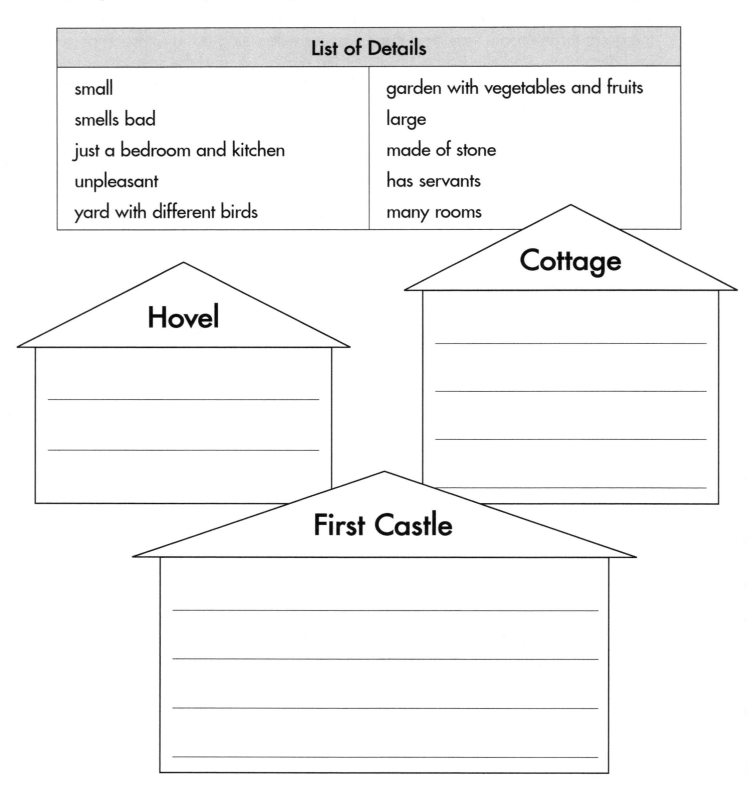

List of Details	
small	garden with vegetables and fruits
smells bad	large
just a bedroom and kitchen	made of stone
unpleasant	has servants
yard with different birds	many rooms

Hovel

Cottage

First Castle

Grade 3 passages and questions with responses for "The Fisherman and His Wife" by Jacob and Wilhelm Grimm, translated by Lucy Crane, reprinted with permission from Student Achievement Partners (2015).

Question 7

Which statement from Scene 3 best shows that the wife treats the husband poorly?

A. "'Husband, get up and just look out of the window.'"
B. "'Well,' said the wife, 'if you don't want to be king, I will be king.'"
C. "'O husband!' said the wife, seeming quite restless, 'I am tired of this already.'"
D. "'Now, look here,' said the wife, 'I am king, and you are only my husband, so will you go at once?'"

Grade 3 passages and questions with responses for "The Fisherman and His Wife" by Jacob and Wilhelm Grimm, translated by Lucy Crane, reprinted with permission from Student Achievement Partners (2015).

SCENE 4:

59 With that he came to the sea, and the water was quite black and thick, and the foam flew, and the wind blew, and the man was terrified. But he stood and said,

> "O man, O man!—if man you be,
> Or flounder, flounder, in the sea—
> Such a tiresome wife I've got,
> For she wants what I do not."

60 "What is it now?" said the fish.

61 "Oh dear!" said the man, "my wife wants to be emperor."

62 "Go home with you," said the fish, "she is emperor already."

63 So the man went home, and found the castle adorned with polished marble and alabaster figures, and golden gates. The troops were being marshalled before the door, and they were blowing trumpets and beating drums and cymbals; and when he entered he saw barons and earls and dukes waiting about like servants; and the doors were of bright gold. And he saw his wife sitting upon a throne made of one entire piece of gold, and it was about two miles high; and she had a great golden crown on, which was about three yards high . . .

64 So the man went up to her and said, "Well, wife, so now you are emperor."

65 "Yes," said she, "now I am emperor."

66 Then he went and sat down and had a good look at her, and then he said, "Well now, wife, there is nothing left to be, now you are emperor."

67 "We will see about that," said the wife. With that they both went to bed; but she was as far as ever from being contented, and she could not get to sleep for thinking of what she should like to be next.

68 The husband, however, slept as fast as a top after his busy day; but the wife tossed and turned from side to side the whole night through, thinking all the while what she could be next, but nothing would occur to her; and when she saw the red dawn she slipped off the bed, and sat before the window to see

Grade 3 passages and questions with responses for "The Fisherman and His Wife" by Jacob and Wilhelm Grimm, translated by Lucy Crane, reprinted with permission from Student Achievement Partners (2015).

the sun rise, and as it came up she said, "Ah, I have it! What if I should make the sun and moon to rise—husband!" she cried, and stuck her elbow in his ribs, "Wake up, and go to your fish, and tell him I want power over the sun and moon."

69 The man was so fast asleep that when he started up he fell out of bed. Then he shook himself together, and opened his eyes and said, "Oh,—wife, what did you say?"

70 "Husband," said she, "if I cannot get the power of making the sun and moon rise when I want them, I shall never have another quiet hour. Go to the fish and tell him so."

71 "O wife!" said the man, and fell on his knees to her, "the fish can really not do that for you. I grant you he could make you emperor . . . do be contented with that, I beg of you."

72 And she became wild with impatience, and screamed out, "I can wait no longer, go at once!"

73 And so off he went as well as he could for fright. And a dreadful storm arose, so that he could hardly keep his feet; and the houses and trees were blown down, and the mountains trembled, and rocks fell in the sea; the sky was quite black, and it thundered and lightened; and the waves, crowned with foam, ran mountains high. So he cried out, without being able to hear his own words,

> "O man, O man!—if man you be,
> Or flounder, flounder, in the sea—
> Such a tiresome wife I've got,
> For she wants what I do not."

74 "Well, what now?" said the flounder.

75 "Oh dear!" said the man, "she wants to order about the sun and moon."

76 "Go home with you!" said the flounder, "you will find her in the old hovel."

77 And there they are sitting to this very day.

Grade 3 passages and questions with responses for "The Fisherman and His Wife" by Jacob and Wilhelm Grimm, translated by Lucy Crane, reprinted with permission from Student Achievement Partners (2015).

Question 8

Which sentence from Scene 4 best shows that the fish has become angry about the situation?

A. "'What is it now?' said the fish."
B. "'Go home with you,' said the fish, 'she is emperor already.'"
C. "'Well, what now?' said the flounder."
D. "'Go home with you!' said the flounder, 'you will find her in the old hovel.'"

Question 9

This question has two parts. First answer Part A and then answer Part B.

Part A

The water changes throughout the scenes of this story. Draw an arrow from the event to the way the water looks when the fisherman makes his request.

Event	Description
The fisherman asks for a cottage for his wife.	The purple, grey, and blue water is thick.
The fisherman asks if his wife can be emperor.	The water forms high, foamy waves that crash into the mountains.
The fisherman asks if his wife can be king.	The water is green and yellow.
The fisherman asks for a castle for his wife.	The dark grey water came up on the land and smelled bad.
The fisherman asks if his wife can have power over the sun and moon.	The water becomes thick, black, and foamy.

Grade 3 passages and questions with responses for "The Fisherman and His Wife" by Jacob and Wilhelm Grimm, translated by Lucy Crane, reprinted with permission from Student Achievement Partners (2015).

Part B

How does the changing water in each scene add to the story?

A. The water shows the emotions of the husband.
B. The water shows the emotions of the wife.
C. The water shows the emotions of the fish.
D. The water shows the emotions of the narrator.

Question 10

The following question has two parts. Answer Part A and then answer Part B.

Part A

What lesson does this story teach?

A. You should be satisfied with what you have.
B. You should be kind to others so you will be rewarded.
C. You should try to make other people happy even if what they ask of you is wrong.
D. You should work hard for what you get so that you take care of it.

Part B

What happened as a result of the wife not learning this lesson?

A. Her husband would no longer help her.
B. She was punished by having to live in a hovel again.
C. Her husband became emperor instead of letting her rule.
D. She caused a terrible storm that destroyed her castle.

Grade 3 passages and questions with responses for "The Fisherman and His Wife" by Jacob and Wilhelm Grimm, translated by Lucy Crane, reprinted with permission from Student Achievement Partners (2015).

Grade 4 Sample Items

Read the following passage.

The Velveteen Rabbit
Or
How Toys Become Real
by Margery Williams
Illustrations by William Nicholson

1   There was once a velveteen rabbit, and in the beginning he was really splendid. He was fat and bunchy, as a rabbit should be; his coat was spotted brown and white, he had real thread whiskers, and his ears were lined with pink sateen. On Christmas morning, when he sat wedged in the top of the Boy's stocking, with a sprig of holly between his paws, the effect was charming.

2   There were other things in the stocking, nuts and oranges and a toy engine, and chocolate almonds and a clockwork mouse, but the Rabbit was quite the best of all. For at least two hours the Boy loved him, and then Aunts and Uncles came to dinner, and there was a great rustling of tissue paper and unwrapping of parcels, and in the excitement of looking at all the new presents the Velveteen Rabbit was forgotten.

Christmas Morning

Christmas morning

Grade 4 passage from *The Velveteen Rabbit Or How Toys Become Real* by Margery Williams. Public Domain. Questions and responses by Adele Macula, EdD.

3 For a long time he lived in the toy cupboard or on the nursery floor, and no one thought very much about him. He was naturally shy, and being only made of velveteen, some of the more expensive toys quite snubbed him.

4 The mechanical toys were very superior, and looked down upon every one else; they were full of modern ideas, and pretended they were real. The model boat, who had lived through two seasons and lost most of his paint, caught the tone from them and never missed an opportunity of referring to his rigging in technical terms.

5 The Rabbit could not claim to be a model of anything, for he didn't know that real rabbits existed; he thought they were all stuffed with sawdust like himself, and he understood that sawdust was quite out-of-date and should never be mentioned in modern circles.

6 Even Timothy, the jointed wooden lion, who was made by the disabled soldiers, and should have had broader views, put on airs and pretended he was connected with Government. Between them all the poor little Rabbit was made to feel himself very insignificant and commonplace, and the only person who was kind to him at all was the Skin Horse.

7 The Skin Horse had lived longer in the nursery than any of the others. He was so old that his brown coat was bald in patches and showed the seams underneath, and most of the hairs in his tail had been pulled out to string bead necklaces. He was wise, for he had seen a long succession of mechanical toys arrive to boast and swagger, and by-and-by break their mainsprings and pass away, and he knew that they were only toys, and would never turn into anything else. For nursery magic is very strange and wonderful, and only those playthings that are old and wise and experienced like the Skin Horse understand all about it.

8 "What is REAL?" asked the Rabbit one day, when they were lying side by side near the nursery fender, before Nana came to tidy the room. "Does it mean having things that buzz inside you and a stick-out handle?"

9 "Real isn't how you are made," said the Skin Horse. "It's a thing that happens to you. When a child loves you for a long, long time, not just to play with, but REALLY loves you, then you become Real."

10 "Does it hurt?" asked the Rabbit.

Grade 4 passage from *The Velveteen Rabbit Or How Toys Become Real* by Margery Williams. Public Domain. Questions and responses by Adele Macula, EdD.

11 "Sometimes," said the Skin Horse, for he was always truthful. "When you are Real you don't mind being hurt."

12 "Does it happen all at once, like being wound up," he asked, "or bit by bit?"

13 "It doesn't happen all at once," said the Skin Horse. "You become. It takes a long time. That's why it doesn't happen often to people who break easily, or have sharp edges, or who have to be carefully kept. Generally, by the time you are Real, most of your hair has been loved off, and your eyes drop out and you get loose in the joints and very shabby. But these things don't matter at all, because once you are Real you can't be ugly, except to people who don't understand."

14 "I suppose you are real?" said the Rabbit. And then he wished he had not said it, for he thought the Skin Horse might be sensitive. But the Skin Horse only smiled.

The Skin Horse Tells His Story

15 "The Boy's Uncle made me Real," he said. "That was a great many years ago; but once you are Real you can't become unreal again. It lasts for always."

16 The Rabbit sighed. He thought it would be a long time before this magic called Real happened to him. He longed to become Real, to know what it felt like; and yet the idea of growing shabby and losing his eyes and whiskers was rather sad. He wished that he could become it without these uncomfortable things happening to him.

17 There was a person called Nana who ruled the nursery. Sometimes she took no notice of the playthings lying about, and sometimes, for no reason whatever, she went swooping about like a great wind and hustled them away in cupboards. She called this "tidying up," and the playthings all hated it, especially the tin ones. The Rabbit didn't mind it so much, for wherever he was thrown he came down soft.

18 One evening, when the Boy was going to bed, he couldn't find the china dog that always slept with him. Nana was in a hurry, and it was too much trouble to hunt for china dogs at bedtime, so she simply looked about her, and seeing that the toy cupboard door stood open, she made a swoop.

19 "Here," she said, "take your old Bunny! He'll do to sleep with you!" And she dragged the Rabbit out by one ear, and put him into the Boy's arms.

Grade 4 passage from *The Velveteen Rabbit Or How Toys Become Real* by Margery Williams. Public Domain. Questions and responses by Adele Macula, EdD.

Question 1

The following question has two parts. Answer Part A and then answer Part B.

Part A

Which sentence from the story helps the reader understand the meaning of "splendid" as it is used in paragraph 1?

A. "There were other things in the stocking, nuts and oranges and a toy engine, and chocolate almonds and a clockwork mouse, but the Rabbit was quite the best of all." (paragraph 2)

B. "He was naturally shy, and being only made of velveteen, some of the more expensive toys quite snubbed him." (paragraph 3)

C. "The Rabbit could not claim to be a model of anything, for he didn't know that real rabbits existed..." (paragraph 5)

D. "Does it happen all at once, like being wound up," he asked, "or bit by bit?" (paragraph 12)

Part B

Which word has the opposite meaning of "splendid"?

A. sugary
B. wonderful
C. quiet
D. average

Grade 4 passage from *The Velveteen Rabbit Or How Toys Become Real* by Margery Williams. Public Domain. Questions and responses by Adele Macula, EdD.

Question 2

Part A

Which statement from the story best shows how the Rabbit thinks of himself?

A. "But these things don't matter at all, because once you are Real you can't be ugly, except to people who don't understand." (paragraph 13)
B. "He thought it would be a long time before this magic called Real happened to him." (paragraph 16)
C. "Between them all the poor little Rabbit was made to feel himself very insignificant and commonplace, and the only person who was kind to him at all was the Skin Horse." (paragraph 6)
D. "And she dragged the Rabbit out by one ear, and put him into the Boy's arms." (paragraph 19)

Part B

Which detail from the story provides evidence for the answer to Part A?

A. "'Real isn't how you are made,' said the Skin Horse. 'It's a thing that happens to you.'" (paragraph 9)
B. "He was naturally shy, and being only made of velveteen, some of the more expensive toys quite snubbed him." (paragraph 3)
C. "He was fat and bunchy, as a rabbit should be; his coat was spotted brown and white, he had real thread whiskers, and his ears were lined with pink sateen." (paragraph 1)
D. "There was a person called Nana who ruled the nursery. Sometimes she took no notice of the playthings lying about, and sometimes, for no reason whatever, she went swooping about like a great wind and hustled them away in cupboards." (paragraph 17)

Grade 4 passage from *The Velveteen Rabbit Or How Toys Become Real* by Margery Williams. Public Domain. Questions and responses by Adele Macula, EdD.

Question 3

Part A

Which sentence describes the Skin Horse and the Rabbit in the story?

A. They feel sadness toward each other.
B. They treat each other with kindness.
C. They do not like each other.
D. They show jealousy toward each other.

Part B

Which detail from the story supports the answer to Part A?

A. "The Skin Horse had lived longer in the nursery than any of the others." (paragraph 7)
B. "'What is REAL?' asked the Rabbit one day, when they were lying side by side near the nursery fender, before Nana came to tidy the room." (paragraph 8)
C. "Generally, by the time you are Real, most of your hair has been loved off, and your eyes drop out and you get loose in the joints and very shabby." (paragraph 13)
D. "Between them all the poor little Rabbit was made to feel himself very insignificant and commonplace, and the only person who was kind to him at all was the Skin Horse." (paragraph 6)

Grade 4 passage from *The Velveteen Rabbit Or How Toys Become Real* by Margery Williams. Public Domain. Questions and responses by Adele Macula, EdD.

Question 4

Part A

Which character trait best describes the Skin Horse?

A. honest
B. bold
C. weak
D. humorous

Part B

Which statement from the story supports the answer to Part A?

A. "Between them all the poor little Rabbit was made to feel himself very insignificant and commonplace, and the only person who was kind to him at all was the Skin Horse." (paragraph 6)
B. "For nursery magic is very strange and wonderful, and only those playthings that are old and wise and experienced like the Skin Horse understand all about it." (paragraph 7)
C. "'Sometimes,' said the Skin Horse, for he was always truthful. 'When you are Real you don't mind being hurt.'" (paragraph 11)
D. "'It doesn't happen all at once,' said the Skin Horse. 'You become. It takes a long time.'" (paragraph 13)

Grade 4 passage from *The Velveteen Rabbit Or How Toys Become Real* by Margery Williams. Public Domain. Questions and responses by Adele Macula, EdD.

Question 5

Part A

Which sentence **best** states a theme in the story?

A. Love makes us feel real.
B. We should try to be patient with others.
C. We all want to be a toy.
D. Being superior over others makes us feel good.

Part B

Which detail from the story **best** shows this theme?

A. "Generally, by the time you are Real, most of your hair has been loved off, and your eyes drop out and you get loose in the joints and very shabby." (paragraph 13)
B. "'When a child loves you for a long, long time, not just to play with, but REALLY loves you, then you become Real.'" (paragraph 9)
C. "For at least two hours the Boy loved him, and then Aunts and Uncles came to dinner..." (paragraph 2)
D. "For a long time he lived in the toy cupboard or on the nursery floor, and no one thought very much about him." (paragraph 3)

Grade 4 passage from *The Velveteen Rabbit Or How Toys Become Real* by Margery Williams. Public Domain. Questions and responses by Adele Macula, EdD.

Grade 5 Sample Items

The Summer of the Swans

The questions in this mini-assessment are based on two excerpts from *The Summer of the Swans,* published by Viking Press, a division of Penguin Putman Publishing. The texts are not included in this document due to permissions denial for Web rights. The user is solely responsible for any permission that may be necessary to reproduce, distribute, or publicly display the text for purposes of the assessment.

Excerpt 1: from *The Summer of the Swans*

by Betsy Byars

The first excerpt begins on page 121 with the words "Charlie awoke" and ends on page 123 with the words "calling his name."

Excerpt 2: from *The Summer of the Swans*

by Betsy Byars

The second excerpt begins on page 124 with the words "At the top" and ends on page 128 with the words "isn't that better?"

Teacher read aloud: Today you will read two excerpts from *The Summer of the Swans,* a novel by Betsy Byars. You will then answer several questions based on the texts.

Grade 5 questions with responses for *The Summer of the Swans* by Betsy Byars reprinted with permission from Student Achievement Partners (2015).

Question 1

The following question has two parts. Answer Part A and then answer Part B.

Part A

In paragraph 2 of Excerpt 1, what is the meaning of the word "frenzy"?

A. an awkward way
B. a crisscrossing pattern
C. a wild and excited manner
D. an exact and planned course

Part B

Which phrase from the text best helps the reader determine the meaning of "frenzy"?

A. "blank spaces that he could never fill in"
B. "kneeling on the ground in helpless pain"
C. "frightened him so much"
D. "turned and run without direction"

Question 2

Excerpt 1 is told from Charlie's point of view. Choose two ways that Charlie's point of view influences the story.

A. The setting of the story is not revealed until late in the excerpt because Charlie himself does not focus on the setting right away.
B. The small details Charlie remembers become more and more important to him than the situation he is in.
C. The conflict is not revealed until the very end of the excerpt because Charlie remains unaware of the problems he is facing.
D. The challenges Charlie faces in his life appear to be more serious than they really are because Charlie does not understand the details of his situation.
E. The reader is unable to learn about Charlie's personality even though he gains some understanding of the difficult condition he is in.
F. The reader remains unaware of what caused Charlie to become lost because Charlie does not remember the cause of upsetting events.

Grade 5 questions with responses for *The Summer of the Swans* by Betsy Byars reprinted with permission from Student Achievement Partners (2015).

Question 3

The following question has two parts. Answer Part A and then answer Part B.

Part A

Excerpt 1 from *The Summer of the Swans* explains two events from Charlie's life, one from his past and one from the present. Compare these events in Box 2 below by choosing details from the text that show how Charlie reacted to each event. Complete Box 2 by writing two details from Box 1 to show how Charlie reacted.

Box 1

Details from the story	
He turns and runs away.	He cries out so someone might hear him.
He is scared to open his eyes.	He returns to his favorite place.
He feels safe.	He forgets to pay attention to his surroundings.
He looks for someone he knows.	

Box 2

Event	Detail 1 showing Charlie's reaction	Detail 2 showing Charlie's reaction
Charlie sees Sara get hurt at the Dairy Queen.		
Charlie is lost and alone.		

Part B

How do the details you chose above help describe Charlie's character?

A. These details show that Charlie has a difficult time focusing on his surroundings.
B. These details highlight that Charlie does not trust other people to help him.
C. These details present Charlie's fear of unknown people and places.
D. These details illustrate that Charlie tends to panic in stressful situations.

Grade 5 questions with responses for *The Summer of the Swans* by Betsy Byars reprinted with permission from Student Achievement Partners (2015).

Question 4

What is the purpose of the phrase "gripped her like steel" in paragraph 19 of Excerpt 2?

A. To emphasize how calm Charlie feels when he sees Sara
B. To emphasize how strong Charlie's emotions are when Sara rescues him
C. To emphasize how fearful Charlie still is after Sara finds him
D. To emphasize how fast Charlie's emotions change after Sara hugs him

Grade 5 questions with responses for *The Summer of the Swans* by Betsy Byars reprinted with permission from Student Achievement Partners (2015).

Question 5

Which statement best expresses one of the themes of Excerpt 2?

A. When people start exploring nature, they find both challenges
   and excitement.
B. When people work together as a team, they can eventually solve problems.
C. When people care deeply about someone, they become determined to
   help them.
D. When people listen to the advice of others, they more easily reach success in
   whatever they do.

Question 6

In what two ways do paragraphs 1–10 of Excerpt 2 contribute to the
development of the plot?

A. These paragraphs show how events caused Charlie to become lost.
B. These paragraphs show the reasons that Sara must find Charlie.
C. These paragraphs show Sara's sense of excitement as she races to Charlie.
D. These paragraphs show the appearance of the ravine in which Charlie
   finds himself.
E. These paragraphs show how strongly Sara feels about the need to
   find Charlie.
F. These paragraphs show how fearful Sara is that she may be injured again.

Grade 5 questions with responses for *The Summer of the Swans* by Betsy Byars
reprinted with permission from Student Achievement Partners (2015).

Question 7

Based on information from both excerpts, which statement best expresses how Charlie and Sara feel about each other?

A. Charlie is afraid of Sara, and Sara is angry that she must find Charlie.
B. Charlie loves Sara, and Sara loves and wants to take care of Charlie.
C. Charlie wants independence from Sara, and Sara is overprotective of Charlie.
D. Charlie feels abandoned by Sara, and Sara believes she caused Charlie to run away.

Grade 5 questions with responses for *The Summer of the Swans* by Betsy Byars reprinted with permission from Student Achievement Partners (2015).

Question 8

Writing Prompt: These two excerpts from *The Summer of the Swans* are written from the perspective of a different sibling about the same event. Using information from both texts, compare and contrast the characters of Sara and Charlie and their reactions to the event. Be sure to use evidence from both texts in your response. Use the space below and additional paper as needed.

Grade 5 questions with responses for *The Summer of the Swans* by Betsy Byars reprinted with permission from Student Achievement Partners (2015).

Grade 6 Sample Items

Read the soliloquy from *As You Like It* (1599) by William Shakespeare.

Jaques' Soliloquy from *As You Like It* (Act II, Scene vii)

by William Shakespeare

All the world's a stage,
And all the men and women merely players;
They have their exits and their entrances,
And one man in his time plays many parts,
His acts being seven ages. At first, the infant,   5
Mewling and puking in the nurse's arms.
Then the whining schoolboy, with his satchel
And shining morning face, creeping like snail
Unwillingly to school. And then the lover,
Sighing like furnace, with a woeful ballad   10
Made to his mistress' eyebrow. Then a soldier,
Full of strange oaths and bearded like the pard,
Jealous in honor, sudden and quick in quarrel,
Seeking the bubble reputation
Even in the cannon's mouth. And then the justice,   15
In fair round belly with good capon lined,
With eyes severe and beard of formal cut,
Full of wise saws and modern instances;
And so he plays his part. The sixth age shifts
Into the lean and slippered pantaloon,   20
With spectacles on nose and pouch on side;
His youthful hose, well saved, a world too wide
For his shrunk shank, and his big manly voice,
Turning again toward childish treble, pipes
And whistles in his sound. Last scene of all,   25
That ends this strange eventful history,
Is second childishness and mere oblivion,
Sans teeth, sans eyes, sans taste, sans everything.

Grade 6 passage with writing prompts for "Jaques' Soliloquy" from *As You Like It* (Act II, Scene vii) by William Shakespeare reprinted with permission from Student Achievement Partners (2015).

Question

Writing Prompt: You work for a company that is creating a series of picture books for young children. Each book in the series will be based upon the poetry of a different famous writer. There will be no words in these books, only pictures, but the company wants the pictures in the book to accurately represent what the author said. The company also wants to choose works that will make children laugh.

Your boss has asked you to read Jacques' soliloquy carefully and then submit your professional opinion on whether or not the company should include it in the series. As you write:

- Be sure to establish a clear position on whether or not Jaques' soliloquy is appropriate for a children's picture book.

- Support your opinion with ample persuasive details to convince your boss that you have thoroughly considered the question and that you are correct.

- Keep in mind that the most convincing arguments address the opposing view and acknowledge its strengths.

_____

_____

_____

_____

_____

_____

_____

_____

_____

_____

Grade 6 passage with writing prompts for "Jaques' Soliloquy" from *As You Like It* (Act II, Scene vii) by William Shakespeare reprinted with permission from Student Achievement Partners (2015).

Grade 7 Sample Items

Read the text passage and answer the questions that follow.

"Whitewashing the Fence" from *Tom Sawyer*
by Mark Twain

1   But Tom's energy did not last. He began to think of the fun he had planned for this day, and his sorrows multiplied. Soon the free boys would come tripping along on all sorts of delicious expeditions, and they would make a world of fun of him for having to work—the very thought of it burnt him like fire. He got out his worldly wealth and examined it—bits of toys, marbles, and trash; enough to buy an exchange of WORK, maybe, but not half enough to buy so much as half an hour of pure freedom. So he returned his straitened means to his pocket, and gave up the idea of trying to buy the boys. At this dark and hopeless moment an inspiration burst upon him! Nothing less than a great, magnificent inspiration.

2   He took up his brush and went tranquilly to work. Ben Rogers hove in sight presently— the very boy, of all boys, whose ridicule he had been dreading. Ben's gait was the hop-skip-and-jump—proof enough that his heart was light and his anticipations high. He was eating an apple, and giving a long, melodious whoop, at intervals, followed by a deep-toned ding-dong-dong, ding-dong-dong, for he was personating a steamboat. As he drew near, he slackened speed, took the middle of the street, leaned far over to starboard and rounded to ponderously and with laborious pomp and circumstance—for he was personating the Big Missouri, and considered himself to be drawing nine feet of water. He was boat and captain and engine-bells combined, so he had to imagine himself standing on his own hurricane-deck giving the orders and executing them:

3   "Stop her, sir! Ting-a-ling-ling!" The headway ran almost out, and he drew up slowly toward the sidewalk. "Ship up to back! Ting-a-ling-ling!" His arms straightened and stiffened down his sides.

4   "Set her back on the stabboard! Ting-a-ling-ling! Chow! ch-chow-wow! Chow!" His right hand, meantime, describing stately circles—for it was representing a forty-foot wheel.

5   "Let her go back on the labboard! Ting-a-lingling! Chow-ch-chow-chow!" The left hand began to describe circles. "Stop the stabboard! Ting-a-ling-ling! Stop the labboard! Come ahead on the stabboard! Stop her! Let your outside turn over slow! Ting-a-ling-ling! Chow-ow-ow! Get out that head-line! LIVELY now! Come—out with your spring-line— what're you about there! Take a turn round that stump with the bight of it! Stand by that stage, now—let her go! Done with the engines, sir! Ting-a-ling-ling! ..." (trying the gauge-cocks)."

Grade 6–8 passage with questions and written responses for "Whitewashing the Fence" from *Tom Sawyer* by Mark Twain reprinted with permission from Student Achievement Partners (2015).]

6 Tom went on whitewashing—paid no attention to the steamboat. Ben stared a moment and then said: "Hi-YI! YOU'RE up a stump, ain't you!"

7 No answer. Tom surveyed his last touch with the eye of an artist, then he gave his brush another gentle sweep and surveyed the result, as before. Ben ranged up alongside of him. Tom's mouth watered for the apple, but he stuck to his work.

8 Ben said: "Hello, old chap, you got to work, hey?"

9 Tom wheeled suddenly and said: "Why, it's you, Ben! I warn't noticing."

10 "Say—I'm going in a-swimming, I am. Don't you wish you could? But of course you'd druther WORK—wouldn't you? Course you would!"

11 Tom contemplated the boy a bit, and said: "What do you call work?"

12 "Why, ain't THAT work?"

13 Tom resumed his whitewashing, and answered carelessly: "Well, maybe it is, and maybe it ain't. All I know, is it suits Tom Sawyer."

14 "Oh come, now, you don't mean to let on that you LIKE it?"

15 The brush continued to move.

16 "Like it? Well, I don't see why I oughtn't to like it. Does a boy get a chance to whitewash a fence every day?" That put the thing in a new light. Ben stopped nibbling his apple. Tom swept his brush daintily back and forth—stepped back to note the effect—added a touch here and there—criticized the effect again—Ben watching every move and getting more and more interested, more and more absorbed. Presently he said:

17 "Say, Tom, let ME whitewash a little."

18 Tom considered, was about to consent; but he altered his mind:

19 "No—no—I reckon it wouldn't hardly do, Ben. You see, Aunt Polly's awful particular about this fence—right here on the street, you know—but if it was the back fence I wouldn't mind and SHE wouldn't. Yes, she's awful particular about this fence; it's got to be done very careful; I reckon there ain't one boy in a thousand, maybe two thousand, that can do it the way it's got to be done."

20 "No—is that so? Oh come now—lemme just try. Only just a little—I'd let YOU, if you was me, Tom."

Grade 6–8 passage with questions and written responses for "Whitewashing the Fence" from *Tom Sawyer* by Mark Twain reprinted with permission from Student Achievement Partners (2015).]

21 "Ben, I'd like to, honest injun; but Aunt Polly—well, Jim wanted to do it, but she wouldn't let him; Sid wanted to do it, and she wouldn't let Sid. Now don't you see how I'm fixed? If you was to tackle this fence and anything was to happen to it—"

22 "Oh, shucks, I'll be just as careful. Now lemme try. Say—I'll give you the core of my apple."

23 "Well, here—No, Ben, now don't. I'm afeard—"

24 "I'll give you ALL of it!"

25 Tom gave up the brush with reluctance in his face, but alacrity in his heart. And while the late steamer Big Missouri worked and sweated in the sun, the retired artist sat on a barrel in the shade close by, dangled his legs, munched his apple, and planned the slaughter of more innocents. There was no lack of material; boys happened along every little while; they came to jeer, but remained to whitewash. By the time Ben was fagged[1] out, Tom had traded the next chance to Billy Fisher for a kite, in good repair; and when he played out, Johnny Miller bought in for a dead rat and a string to swing it with—and so on, and so on, hour after hour. And when the middle of the afternoon came, from being a poor poverty-stricken boy in the morning, Tom was literally rolling in wealth. He had besides the things before mentioned, twelve marbles, part of a jews-harp, a piece of blue bottle-glass to look through, a spool cannon, a key that wouldn't unlock anything, a fragment of chalk, a glass stopper of a decanter, a tin soldier, a couple of tadpoles, six fire-crackers, a kitten with only one eye, a brass doorknob, a dog-collar—but no dog—the handle of a knife, four pieces of orange-peel, and a dilapidated old window sash.

26 He had had a nice, good, idle time all the while—plenty of company—and the fence had three coats of whitewash on it! If he hadn't run out of whitewash he would have bankrupted every boy in the village.

27 Tom said to himself that it was not such a hollow world, after all. He had discovered a great law of human action, without knowing it—namely, that in order to make a man or a boy covet a thing, it is only necessary to make the thing difficult to attain. If he had been a great and wise philosopher, like the writer of this book, he would now have comprehended that Work consists of whatever a body is OBLIGED to do, and that Play consists of whatever a body is not obliged to do. And this would help him to understand why constructing artificial flowers or performing on a tread-mill is work, while rolling ten-pins or climbing Mont Blanc is only amusement. There are wealthy gentlemen in England who drive four-horse passenger-coaches twenty or thirty miles on a daily line, in the summer, because the privilege costs them considerable money; but if they were offered wages for the service, that would turn it into work and then they would resign.

28 The boy mused awhile over the substantial change which had taken place in his worldly circumstances, and then wended toward headquarters to report.

[1] Made tired by hard work

Grade 6–8 passage with questions and written responses for "Whitewashing the Fence" from *Tom Sawyer* by Mark Twain reprinted with permission from Student Achievement Partners (2015).]

Question 1

Tom's "great, magnificent inspiration" in paragraph 1 is important to developing the plot of the story. What is Tom's inspiration?

A. He develops a plan for tricking the other boys into doing most of his work.
B. He decides to bribe the boys with his "worldly wealth" in order to get the boys to paint the fence.
C. He thinks of ways to make himself enjoy the task of painting the fence.
D. He focuses on the exciting things around him to distract himself from his work.
E. He asks his friends to help him so they can all go swimming together.

Question 2

In "Whitewashing the Fence," the author writes Tom and Ben's dialogue using dialect, a special variety of language that includes misspelling and informal words, to

A. build suspense about what will happen next.
B. help establish the rural nature of the setting.
C. establish a conflict between Tom and Ben.
D. help characterize Tom and Ben as ignorant.
E. make a point about human nature.

Grade 6–8 passage with questions and written responses for "Whitewashing the Fence" from *Tom Sawyer* by Mark Twain reprinted with permission from Student Achievement Partners (2015).]

Question 3

In paragraph 1, the author uses phrases like "free boys," "delicious expeditions," and "pure freedom" to suggest that

A. Tom resents his aunt for making him work.
B. Tom believes he should not be made to do chores.
C. Tom is tired from working so hard on the fence.
D. Tom highly values time spent having fun.
E. Tom thinks the task of painting the fence is enjoyable.

Question 4

This question has two parts. Answer part A and then answer part B.

Part A

How do paragraphs 2 through 6, in which Ben pretends to be a steamboat, contribute to the development of the passage?

A. They emphasize the many distractions Tom faces.
B. They hint at Tom's plan for getting his work done.
C. They highlight the friendship between Tom and Ben.
D. They foreshadow the fact Ben will soon be working.
E. They characterize Ben as someone who likes to show off.

Part B

What event in the passage results from the answer to Part A?

A. Tom focuses on painting the fence instead of choosing to play.
B. Tom tells his friend why he likes whitewashing.
C. Tom tricks Ben into choosing to whitewash the fence instead of playing.
D. Tom gets many boys to paint the fence.

Grade 6–8 passage with questions and written responses for "Whitewashing the Fence" from Tom Sawyer by Mark Twain reprinted with permission from Student Achievement Partners (2015).]

Question 5

This question has two parts. Answer part A and then answer part B.

Part A

Which two statements best express the reasons for Tom's success in getting the other boys to do his work for him?

A. Tom has the ability to keep his true feelings hidden.

B. Tom is popular with others and a natural leader.

C. Tom accepts that some situations are beyond his control.

D. Tom dislikes thinking people will make fun of him.

E. Tom understands how to make people feel envious.

F. Tom values objects that other people might view as junk.

Part B

Which excerpt from the passage provides the best evidence for the answers to Part A?

A. "Soon the free boys would come tripping along on all sorts of delicious expeditions, and they would make a world of fun of him for having to work—the very thought of it burnt him like fire."

B. "He got out his worldly wealth and examined it—bits of toys, marbles, and trash; enough to buy an exchange of WORK, maybe, but not half enough to buy so much as half an hour of pure freedom."

C. "'Like it? Well, I don't see why I oughtn't to like it. Does a boy get a chance to whitewash a fence every day?' That put the thing in a new light."

D. "And when the middle of the afternoon came, from being a poor poverty-stricken boy in the morning, Tom was literally rolling in wealth."

E. "He had discovered a great law of human action, without knowing it—namely, that in order to make a man or a boy covet a thing, it is only necessary to make the thing difficult to attain."

Grade 6–8 passage with questions and written responses for "Whitewashing the Fence" from *Tom Sawyer* by Mark Twain reprinted with permission from Student Achievement Partners (2015).]

Question 6

To convince Ben that Ben should want to whitewash the fence, Tom shows Ben that whitewashing is a rewarding experience and requires special skill.

In each of the boxes below, find the one paragraph in which Tom conveys each idea about whitewashing. Highlight the paragraph in the text and copy the entire paragraph into the box.

"Whitewashing is a rewarding experience."

```


```

"Whitewashing requires special skill."

```


```

Grade 6–8 passage with questions and written responses for "Whitewashing the Fence" from *Tom Sawyer* by Mark Twain reprinted with permission from Student Achievement Partners (2015).]

Question 7

This question has two parts. Answer part A and then answer part B.

Part A

Which statement best expresses the main theme of "Whitewashing the Fence"?

A. Friends make sacrifices to help each other.

B. People often value things that seem hard to get.

C. Work can be enjoyable if one has the right attitude.

D. Time is more precious than money or material goods.

Part B

Which lines from the passage does the author provide to best illustrate this theme?

A. "Tom surveyed his last touch with the eye of an artist, then he gave his brush another gentle sweep and surveyed the result, as before."

B. "'Say—I'm going in a-swimming, I am. Don't you wish you could? But of course you'd druther WORK—wouldn't you? Course you would!'"

C. "He had discovered a great law of human action, without knowing it—namely, that in order to make a man or a boy covet a thing, it is only necessary to make the thing difficult to attain."

D. "He had besides the things before mentioned, twelve marbles, part of a jews-harp, a piece of blue bottle-glass to look through, a spool cannon, a key that wouldn't unlock anything, a fragment of chalk, a glass stopper of a decanter, a tin soldier, a couple of tadpoles, six fire-crackers, a kitten with only one eye, a brass doorknob, a dog-collar— but no dog—the handle of a knife, four pieces of orange-peel, and a dilapidated old window sash."

Grade 6–8 passage with questions and written responses for "Whitewashing the Fence" from *Tom Sawyer* by Mark Twain reprinted with permission from Student Achievement Partners (2015).]

Question 8: Writing Task

Writing Prompt 1: Construct a narrative that teaches the same lesson(s) that Tom learns at the end of the passage. Incorporate both the voice of a narrator as well as dialogue in your story. Use additional paper to complete the writing task.

_____

_____

_____

_____

_____

_____

_____

_____

Writing Prompt 2: Write a parody of the scene by changing the characters and work being done to reflect a modern dilemma. Use additional paper to complete the writing task.

_____

_____

_____

_____

_____

_____

_____

_____

Grade 7 Sample Items

Read the text passage.

Narrative of the Life of Frederick Douglass, an American Slave, Written by Himself (1845)

by Frederick Douglass

Exemplar Text	Vocabulary
The plan which I adopted, and the one by which I was most successful, was that of making friends of all the little white boys whom I met in the street. As many of these as I could, I **converted** into teachers. With their kindly aid, obtained at different times and in different places, I finally succeeded in learning to read. When I was sent on errands, I always took my book with me, and by going on one part of my <u>errand</u> quickly, I found time to get a lesson before my return. I used also to carry bread with me, enough of which was always in the house, and to which I was always welcome; for I was much better off in this regard than many of the poor white children in our neighborhood. This bread I used to <u>bestow</u> upon the hungry little **urchins**, who, in return, would give me that more valuable bread of knowledge. I am strongly **tempted** to give the names of two or three of those little boys, as a **testimonial** of the <u>gratitude</u> and affection I bear them; but <u>prudence</u> forbids;—not that it would injure me, but it might embarrass them; for it is almost an **unpardonable** offence to teach slaves to read in this Christian country. It is enough to say of the dear little fellows, that they lived on Philpot Street, very near Durgin and Bailey's <u>ship-yard</u>. I used to talk this matter of slavery over with them. I would sometimes say to them, I wished I could be as free as they would be when they got to be men. "You will be free as soon as you are twenty-one, but I am a slave for life! Have not I as good a right to be free as you have?" These words used to trouble them; they would express for me the **liveliest sympathy**, and **console** me with the hope that something would occur by which I might be free.	*chore (singular)* *give* *to show of thankfulness; state of being wise and careful* *place where ships are repaired or built*

Grade 7 passage with writing prompts from *Narrative of the Life of Frederick Douglass, an American Slave, Written by Himself* (1845) by Frederick Douglass reprinted with permission from Student Achievement Partners (2015).

Exemplar Text	Vocabulary
I was now about twelve years old, and the thought of being a slave for life began **to bear** heavily upon my heart. Just about this time, I got hold of a book entitled "The Columbian <u>Orator</u>." Every opportunity I got, I used to read this book. Among much of other interesting matter, I found in it a **dialogue** between a master and his slave. The slave was represented as having run away from his master three times. The dialogue represented the conversation which took place between them, when the slave was retaken the third time. In this dialogue, the whole argument in **behalf** of slavery was brought forward by the master, all of which was <u>disposed</u> of by the slave. The slave was made to say some very smart as well as impressive things in reply to his master—things which had the desired though unexpected effect; for the conversation resulted in the voluntary <u>emancipation</u> of the slave on the part of the master.	*speaker* *thrown out* *release*

Grade 7 passage with writing prompts from *Narrative of the Life of Frederick Douglass, an American Slave, Written by Himself* (1845) by Frederick Douglass reprinted with permission from Student Achievement Partners (2015).

Exemplar Text	Vocabulary
In the same book, I met with one of Sheridan's mighty speeches on and in behalf of <u>Catholic emancipation</u>. These were choice documents to me. I read them over and over again with **unabated** interest. They gave tongue to interesting thoughts of my own soul, which had frequently flashed through my mind, and died away for want of <u>utterance</u>. The moral which I gained from the dialogue was the power of truth over the conscience of even a slaveholder. What I got from Sheridan was a bold <u>denunciation</u> of slavery, and a powerful **vindication** of human rights. The reading of these documents **enabled** me to utter my thoughts, and to meet the arguments brought forward to <u>sustain</u> slavery; but while they relieved me of one difficulty, they brought on another even more painful than the one of which I was relieved. The more I read, the more I was led to <u>abhor</u> and **detest** my enslavers. I could regard them in no other light than a band of successful robbers, who had left their homes, and gone to Africa, and stolen us from our homes, and in a strange land reduced us to slavery. I **loathed** them as being the meanest as well as the most wicked of men. As I read and **contemplated** the subject, behold! that very discontentment which Master Hugh had predicted would follow my learning to read had already come, to **torment** and sting my soul to unutterable **anguish**. As I <u>writhed</u> under it, I would at times feel that learning to read had been a curse rather than a blessing. It had given me a view of my <u>wretched</u> condition, without the **remedy**. It opened my eyes to the horrible pit, but to no ladder upon which to get out. In moments of agony, I envied my fellow-slaves for their stupidity. I have often wished myself a beast. I preferred the condition of the meanest reptile to my own. Any thing, no matter what, to get rid of thinking! It was this everlasting thinking of my condition that tormented me. There was no getting rid of it. It was pressed upon me by every object within sight or hearing, <u>animate</u> or inanimate. The silver <u>trump</u> of freedom had **roused** my soul to **eternal** wakefulness. Freedom now appeared, to disappear no more forever. It was heard in every sound, and seen in every thing. It was ever present to torment me with a sense of my wretched condition. I saw nothing without seeing it, I heard nothing without hearing it, and felt nothing without feeling it. It looked from every star, it smiled in every calm, breathed in every wind, and moved in every storm.	*a movement to allow Catholics to have full rights* *speaking out loud* *publicly condemn* *keep alive* *hate* *squirmed or struggled; miserable* *alive; resource or advantage more important than any other (short for trumpet)*

Grade 7 passage with writing prompts from *Narrative of the Life of Frederick Douglass, an American Slave, Written by Himself* (1845) by Frederick Douglass reprinted with permission from Student Achievement Partners (2015).

Question 1

Writing Prompt: How do Douglass' feelings change over the course of this piece? What is Douglass trying to show about how slavery makes people feel? Write a paragraph in which you show how his feelings change and what you believe he is trying to show the reader. Use additional paper to complete the writing task.

_____

_____

_____

_____

_____

_____

_____

_____

_____

_____

_____

_____

_____

_____

_____

_____

Grade 7 passage with writing prompts from *Narrative of the Life of Frederick Douglass, an American Slave, Written by Himself* (1845) by Frederick Douglass reprinted with permission from Student Achievement Partners (2015).

Question 2

Writing Prompt: Write about where in the text you see evidence that Douglass is consciously crafting his narrative to present a particular point of view. You should choose passages you feel present evidence of intentional crafting in word choice. Use additional paper to complete the writing task.

_____

_____

_____

_____

_____

_____

_____

_____

_____

_____

_____

_____

_____

_____

_____

_____

_____

_____

Grade 7 passage with writing prompts from _Narrative of the Life of Frederick Douglass, an American Slave, Written by Himself_ (1845) by Frederick Douglass reprinted with permission from Student Achievement Partners (2015).

Grade 8 Sample Items

Read the excerpt from *The Open Boat,* a short story by Stephen Crane.

Chapter III
from *The Open Boat*
by Stephen Crane

1   It would be difficult to describe the subtle brotherhood of men that was here established on the seas. No one said that it was so. No one mentioned it. But it dwelt in the boat, and each man felt it warm him.

2   They were a captain, an oiler, a cook, and a correspondent, and they were friends, friends in a more curiously iron-bound degree than may be common. The hurt captain, lying against the water-jar in the bow, spoke always in a low voice and calmly, but he could never command a more ready and swiftly obedient crew than the motley three of the dinghy. It was more than a mere recognition of what was best for the common safety. There was surely in it a quality that was personal and heartfelt. And after this devotion to the commander of the boat there was this comradeship that the correspondent, for instance, who had been taught to be cynical of men, knew even at the time was the best experience of his life. But no one said that it was so. No one mentioned it.

3   "I wish we had a sail," remarked the captain. "We might try my overcoat on the end of an oar and give you two boys a chance to rest." So the cook and the correspondent held the mast and spread wide the overcoat. The oiler steered, and the little boat made good way with her new rig. Sometimes the oiler had to scull sharply to keep a sea from breaking into the boat, but otherwise sailing was a success.

4   Meanwhile the lighthouse had been growing slowly larger. It had now almost assumed color, and appeared like a little grey shadow on the sky. The man at the oars could not be prevented from turning his head rather often to try for a glimpse of this little grey shadow.

5   At last, from the top of each wave the men in the tossing boat could see land. Even as the lighthouse was an upright shadow on the sky, this land seemed but a long black shadow on the sea. It certainly was thinner than paper. "We must be about opposite New Smyrna," said the cook, who had coasted this shore often in schooners. "Captain, by the way, I believe they abandoned that life-saving station there about a year ago."

6   "Did they?" said the captain.

Grade 8 passage and questions with responses from Chapter III from *The Open Boat* by Stephen Crane reprinted with permission from Student Achievement Partners (2015).

7   The wind slowly died away. The cook and the correspondent were not now obliged to slave in order to hold high the oar. But the waves continued their old impetuous swooping at the dinghy, and the little craft, no longer under way, struggled woundily over them. The oiler or the correspondent took the oars again.

8   Shipwrecks are apropos of nothing. If men could only train for them and have them occur when the men had reached pink condition, there would be less drowning at sea. Of the four in the dinghy none had slept any time worth mentioning for two days and two nights previous to embarking in the dinghy, and in the excitement of clambering about the deck of a foundering ship they had also forgotten to eat heartily.

9   For these reasons, and for others, neither the oiler nor the correspondent was fond of rowing at this time. The correspondent wondered ingenuously how in the name of all that was sane could there be people who thought it amusing to row a boat. It was not an amusement; it was a diabolical punishment, and even a genius of mental aberrations could never conclude that it was anything but a horror to the muscles and a crime against the back. He mentioned to the boat in general how the amusement of rowing struck him, and the weary-faced oiler smiled in full sympathy. Previously to the foundering, by the way, the oiler had worked double-watch in the engine-room of the ship.

10   "Take her easy, now, boys," said the captain. "Don't spend yourselves. If we have to run a surf you'll need all your strength, because we'll sure have to swim for it. Take your time."

11   Slowly the land arose from the sea. From a black line it became a line of black and a line of white, trees and sand. Finally, the captain said that he could make out a house on the shore. "That's the house of refuge, sure," said the cook. "They'll see us before long, and come out after us."

12   The distant lighthouse reared high. "The keeper ought to be able to make us out now, if he's looking through a glass," said the captain. "He'll notify the life-saving people."

13   "None of those other boats could have got ashore to give word of the wreck," said the oiler, in a low voice. "Else the lifeboat would be out hunting us."

14   Slowly and beautifully the land loomed out of the sea. The wind came again. It had veered from the north-east to the south-east. Finally, a new sound struck the ears of the men in the boat. It was the low thunder of the surf on the shore. "We'll never be able to make the lighthouse now," said the captain. "Swing her head a little more north, Billie," said he.

Grade 8 passage and questions with responses from Chapter III from *The Open Boat* by Stephen Crane reprinted with permission from Student Achievement Partners (2015).

15 "A little more north, sir," said the oiler.

16 Whereupon the little boat turned her nose once more down the wind, and all but the oarsman watched the shore grow. Under the influence of this expansion doubt and direful apprehension was leaving the minds of the men. The management of the boat was still most absorbing, but it could not prevent a quiet cheerfulness. In an hour, perhaps, they would be ashore.

17 Their backbones had become thoroughly used to balancing in the boat, and they now rode this wild colt of a dinghy like circus men. The correspondent thought that he had been drenched to the skin, but happening to feel in the top pocket of his coat, he found therein eight cigars. Four of them were soaked with sea-water; four were perfectly scatheless. After a search, somebody produced three dry matches, and thereupon the four waifs rode impudently in their little boat, and with an assurance of an impending rescue shining in their eyes, puffed at the big cigars and judged well and ill of all men. Everybody took a drink of water.

Grade 8 passage and questions with responses from Chapter III from *The Open Boat* by Stephen Crane reprinted with permission from Student Achievement Partners (2015).

Question 1

Choose two ways that the harsh conditions and remote location of the setting contribute to the theme of the passage.

A. They symbolize the characters' desire for freedom and adventure.

B. They provide conflict that propels the action and character development in the story.

C. They allow the author to focus on the environment rather than character development.

D. They permit the author to illustrate the basic principles used to navigate the sea.

E. They help explain the need for cooperation among the men.

F. They illustrate why some members of the crew struggle more than others.

Question 2

Paragraph 1 includes these two sentences: "No one said that it was so. No one mentioned it." Paragraph 2 then includes the same sentences. What is the most likely reason that these sentences are repeated in both paragraphs?

A. The sentences show that there is a limited amount of conversation among the crew members.

B. The sentences show that there is an unspoken level of tension among the crew members.

C. The sentences show that the crew members feel similarly about their situation, and they have formed a strong bond that allows them to leave some thoughts unspoken.

D. The sentences show that although the crew members are outwardly optimistic, they have serious doubts about their survival and keep their doubts to themselves.

Grade 8 passage and questions with responses from Chapter III from *The Open Boat* by Stephen Crane reprinted with permission from Student Achievement Partners (2015).

Question 3

In Paragraph 9, the correspondent reflects on how he views rowing as opposed to how others may view the activity. What is the intended impact of this reflection?

A. It is meant to make the reader pity the correspondent and his current physical state.

B. It is meant to add humor for the reader by injecting the correspondent's wit.

C. It is meant to enlighten the reader about what the correspondent's life was like before.

D. It is meant to encourage the reader to appreciate the correspondent more than the other characters.

Question 4

Which two sentences from the story add suspense by showing that some characters have doubts that they will be rescued?

A. "The hurt captain, lying against the water-jar in the bow, spoke always in a low voice and calmly, but he could never command a more ready and swiftly obedient crew than the motley three of the dinghy." (paragraph 2)

B. "'We might try my overcoat on the end of an oar and give you two boys a chance to rest.'" (paragraph 3)

C. "'Captain, by the way, I believe they abandoned that life-saving station there about a year ago.'" (paragraph 5)

D. "The cook and the correspondent were not now obliged to slave in order to hold high the oar." (paragraph 7)

E. "Of the four in the dinghy none had slept any time worth mentioning for two days and two nights previous to embarking in the dinghy, and in the excitement of clambering about the deck of a foundering ship they had also forgotten to eat heartily." (paragraph 8)

F. "'None of those other boats could have got ashore to give word of the wreck,' said the oiler, in a low voice." (paragraph 13)

Grade 8 passage and questions with responses from Chapter III from *The Open Boat* by Stephen Crane reprinted with permission from Student Achievement Partners (2015).

Question 5

The following question has two parts. Answer Part A and then answer Part B.

Part A

In paragraph 17, what does the phrase "impending rescue" mean?

A. A rescue occurring against many odds
B. A rescue organized according to rules
C. A rescue involving many people
D. A rescue happening soon

Part B

Which sentence from the passage provides the best clue for the meaning of the phrase "impending rescue"?

A. "For these reasons, and for others, neither the oiler nor the correspondent was fond of rowing at this time." (paragraph 9)
B. "'We'll never be able to make the lighthouse now,' said the captain." (paragraph 14)
C. "In an hour, perhaps, they would be ashore." (paragraph 16)
D. "Their backbones had become thoroughly used to balancing in the boat, and they now rode this wild colt of a dinghy like circus men." (paragraph 17)

Grade 8 passage and questions with responses from Chapter III from *The Open Boat* by Stephen Crane reprinted with permission from Student Achievement Partners (2015).

Question 6

From the list of possible conclusions below, choose three conclusions that can be drawn from evidence in the passage and drag them into Column 1. Next, in Column 2, type in the number of the paragraph that provides evidence for each conclusion you've written in Column 1.

The oiler has taken charge of the dinghy.

The men have established a deep respect for the others in the dinghy.

The captain knows his crew thinks they will die on the sea.

The men are weakened from a lack of water.

The men had become friends before embarking in the dinghy.

Rations are limited but shared equally.

The men offer encouragement by promoting thoughts of rescue.

Column 1: Conclusions	Column 2: Number of the paragraph that provides evidence

Grade 8 passage and questions with responses from Chapter III from *The Open Boat* by Stephen Crane reprinted with permission from Student Achievement Partners (2015).

193

Question 7

Writing Prompt: Describe the relationship among the four men in the boat and explain how this relationship is central to the theme and plot of the passage. Be sure to include evidence from the text to support your response. Use additional paper to complete the writing task.

_____

_____

_____

_____

_____

_____

_____

_____

_____

_____

_____

_____

_____

_____

_____

_____

_____

Grade 8 passage and questions with responses from Chapter III from *The Open Boat* by Stephen Crane reprinted with permission from Student Achievement Partners (2015).

Grade 8 Sample Items

Read the poem "Dulce et Decorum Est" by Wilfred Owen. You will then answer several questions based on the poem.

"Dulce et Decorum Est"
by Wilfred Owen

Bent double, like old beggars under sacks,
Knock-kneed, coughing like hags, we cursed through sludge,
Till on the haunting flares we turned our backs,
And towards our distant rest began to trudge.
5   Men marched asleep. Many had lost their boots,
But limped on, blood-shod. All went lame, all blind;
Drunk with fatigue; deaf even to the hoots
Of gas-shells dropping softly behind.

Gas! GAS! Quick, boys! - An ecstasy of fumbling
10   Fitting the clumsy helmets just in time,
But someone still was yelling out and stumbling
And flound'ring like a man in fire or lime. —
Dim through the misty panes and thick green light,
As under a green sea, I saw him drowning.
15   In all my dreams before my helpless sight
He plunges at me, guttering, choking, drowning.
If in some smothering dreams, you too could pace

Behind the wagon that we flung him in,
And watch the white eyes writhing in his face,
20   His hanging face, like a devil's sick of sin,
If you could hear, at every jolt, the blood
Come gargling from the froth-corrupted lungs
Obscene as cancer, bitter as the cud
Of vile, incurable sores on innocent tongues, —
25   My friend, you would not tell with such high zest
To children ardent for some desperate glory,
The old Lie: *Dulce et decorum est*
Pro patria mori. [1]

[1] Literal translation: It is sweet and right to die for your country.

Grade 8 passage and questions with responses from "Dulce et Decorum Est" by Wilfred Owen and "Who's for the Game?" by Jessie Pope reprinted with permission from Student Achievement Partners (2015).

Question 1

The following question has two parts. Answer Part A and then answer Part B.

Part A

What do the first four lines of stanza 1 suggest about the current situation of the soldiers?

A. They have come to depend upon each other for their continued survival.
B. They are depressed because they failed to achieve the day's objectives.
C. They have been at war so long that they can barely remember their former lives.
D. They are retreating to their camp to escape the fighting.

Part B

What does stanza 3 show about the soldiers' situation?

A. The soldiers are not really able to leave the battle behind.
B. The soldiers learn to fend for themselves during a crisis.
C. The soldiers are capable of doing what they have to do.
D. The soldiers are so weary that their mental state is affected.

Grade 8 passage and questions with responses from "Dulce et Decorum Est" by Wilfred Owen and "Who's for the Game?" by Jessie Pope reprinted with permission from Student Achievement Partners (2015).

Question 2

The following question has two parts. Answer Part A and then answer Part B.

Part A

Based on stanza 1, which words **best** describe the soldiers?

A. Lonely and frightened
B. Weak and exhausted
C. Angry and resentful
D. Sad and regretful

Part B

Which three phrases from stanza 1 **best** support the answer to Part A?

A. "Bent double"
B. "cursed through sludge"
C. "haunting flares"
D. "turned our backs"
E. "marched asleep"
F. "drunk with fatigue"
G. "dropping softly behind"

Question 3

The following question has two parts. Answer Part A and then answer Part B.

Part A

Circle two adjoining lines of the poem that show where the speaker begins to focus on the present rather than the past.

(Student will circle two adjoining lines in the poem. Online: Student will highlight text in the poem.)

Part B

What do these two lines best reveal about the speaker?

A. He wishes he had tried harder to help the man who was gassed.
B. He has developed new and intense fears because of the war.
C. He will likely never fully recover from what he endured in the war.
D. He sometimes cannot tell the difference between reality and fantasy.

Question 4

What shift occurs in stanza 4?

A. The timeline advances to after the war to show the effects the experience had on the speaker.
B. The speaker introduces a conflicting point of view and then presents an argument to counter it.
C. The point of view changes so that the speaker is addressing the reader directly.
D. The scene changes from events that actually occurred to events the speaker imagines.

Grade 8 passage and questions with responses from "Dulce et Decorum Est" by Wilfred Owen and "Who's for the Game?" by Jessie Pope reprinted with permission from Student Achievement Partners (2015).

Question 5

The following question has two parts. Answer Part A and then answer Part B.

Part A

Think about how the three longer stanzas (1, 2, and 4) function in the poem. Then complete the chart by writing in (online: dragging and dropping) functions from the list below to their proper place on the chart. One function applies to all three stanzas and should appear on the chart three times. The other functions will each appear once.

The Functions of Each Stanza

	stanza 1	stanza 2	stanza 4
1.			
2.			
3.			

Functions:

Builds tone by telling horrific details

Establishes the war scene

Propels the action of the poem

Introduces the speaker of the poem

States the speaker's view of war

Characterizes the soldiers as weary

Part B

How do stanzas 1, 2, and 4 work together to develop the theme of the poem?

A. By detailing both everyday misery and an agonizing death, the poem suggests that enduring the horrors of war is not wonderful or patriotic.

B. By considering how war affects both individuals and groups of men, the poem suggests that not everyone is fit to fight in battle.

C. By focusing on an unexpected and sudden event, the poem suggests that there is no good way to prepare for one's own death.

D. By describing negative things about being a soldier, the poem suggests that war is ineffective in resolving conflicts between nations.

Grade 8 passage and questions with responses from "Dulce et Decorum Est" by Wilfred Owen and "Who's for the Game?" by Jessie Pope reprinted with permission from Student Achievement Partners (2015).

Question 6

Which statement best summarizes the central idea of this poem?

A. It is one's patriotic duty to fight for one's country, regardless of how unpleasant the consequences.
B. Those who praise war and promote the involvement of young people are promoting a false image of glory.
C. Engaging in war involves tremendous sacrifice and bravery for the public good.
D. All possible methods of resolving conflict should be pursued before young people are asked to fight for their country.

Question 7

In what three ways does this poem challenge or disagree with the idea that to die for your country is a noble thing to do?

A. It treats the outcome of a battle as less important than soldiers' experiences.
B. It shows the pain soldiers feel when society does not appreciate their sacrifices.
C. It portrays soldiers as essentially powerless.
D. It suggests that men are forced to become soldiers against their will.
E. It implies that soldiers who are truly brave do not care about making sacrifices.
F. It establishes that the ancient Romans were the last true soldiers.
G. It denies the possibility of soldiers dying with dignity.

Grade 8 passage and questions with responses from "Dulce et Decorum Est" by Wilfred Owen and "Who's for the Game?" by Jessie Pope reprinted with permission from Student Achievement Partners (2015).

Question 8: Writing Task

Read the statement about Wilfred Owen and then read the poem below. You will compose a written essay based on the writing prompt below.

Wilfred Owen wrote "Dulce et Decorum Est" as a contrast to the poem below, which was written to spur young men to join the war efforts.

Who's for the Game?

by Jessie Pope

Who's for the game, the biggest that's played,
The red crashing game of a fight?
Who'll grip and tackle the job unafraid?
And who thinks he'd rather sit tight?
Who'll toe the line for the signal to 'Go!'?
Who'll give his country a hand?
Who wants a turn to himself in the show?
And who wants a seat in the stand?
Who knows it won't be a picnic—not much—
Yet eagerly shoulders a gun?
Who would much rather come back with a crutch
Than lie low and be out of the fun?
Come along, lads—
But you'll come on all right—
For there's only one course to pursue,
Your country is up to her neck in a fight,
And she's looking and calling for you.

Question 8: Writing Task Continued

Writing Prompt: In "Dulce et Decorum Est" and "Who's for the Game?," each poet presents a strong point of view about war. Write an essay comparing how each poet develops the point of view and what effect each poem is intended to have on the reader. Use textual evidence from both poems to help develop your response. Use additional paper to complete the writing task.

_____

_____

_____

_____

_____

_____

_____

_____

_____

_____

_____

_____

_____

_____

_____

_____

_____

_____

_____

_____

Grade 8 passage and questions with responses from "Dulce et Decorum Est" by Wilfred Owen and "Who's for the Game?" by Jessie Pope reprinted with permission from Student Achievement Partners (2015).

Answer Key

Answers are included for questions that include multiple choice, tables, or short responses to literature.

Grade 3 Sample Items: "The Fisherman and His Wife"

Question 1, Part A: C.

Question 1, Part B: B.

Question 2: A.

Question 3, Part A: D.

Question 3, Part B: B.

Question 4, Part A: C.

Question 4, Part B: A.

Question 5, Part A: B.

Question 5, Part B: A.

Question 6:

House	Answer	Rationale*
Hovel	smells bad unpleasant	According to paragraph 9, the wife says that it is "dreadful" to live in an "evil-smelling hovel."
Cottage	small yard with different birds garden with vegetables and fruits just a bedroom and kitchen	According to paragraph 16, the cottage is described as "a little house-place and a beautiful little bedroom, a kitchen and larder" with "a little garden full of green vegetables and fruit."
First Castle	large made of stone has servants many rooms	According to paragraphs 31 and 32, there appeared "a great castle of stone" with "a great many servants" and "all the rooms had carpets."

*Direct students back to the text to locate the correct answer, if necessary.

Question 7: D.

Question 8: D.

Question 9, Part A:

Event	Description	*Rationale
The fisherman asks for a cottage for his wife.	The water is green and yellow.	According to paragraph 10, "the sea was green and yellow, and not nearly so clear."
The fisherman asks if his wife can be emperor.	The water becomes thick, black, and foamy.	According to paragraph 59, "the water was quite black and thick, and the foam flew, and the wind blew."
The fisherman asks if his wife can be king.	The dark grey water came up on the land and smelled bad.	According to paragraph 44, "the water was quite dark grey, and rushed far inland, and had an ill smell."
The fisherman asks for a castle for his wife.	The purple, grey, and blue water is thick.	According to paragraph 27, "the water was purple and dark blue and grey and thick."
The fisherman asks if his wife can have power over the sun and moon.	The water forms high, foamy waves that crash into the mountains.	According to paragraph 73, "the waves, crowned with foam, ran mountains high."

*Direct students back to the text to locate the correct answer, if necessary.

Question 9, Part B: C.

Question 10, Part A: A.

Question 10, Part B: B.

Grade 4 Sample Items: *The Velveteen Rabbit Or How Toys Become Real*

Question 1, Part A: A.

Question 1, Part B: D.

Question 2, Part A: C.

Question 2, Part B: B.

Question 3, Part A: B.

Question 3, Part B: D.

Question 4, Part A: A.

Question 4, Part B: C.

Question 5, Part A: A.

Question 5, Part B: B.

Grade 5 Sample Items: *The Summer of the Swans*

Question 1, Part A: C.

Question 1, Part B: D.

Question 2: A. and F.

Question 3, Part A:

Event	Detail 1 showing Charlie's reaction	Detail 2 showing Charlie's reaction
Charlie sees Sara get hurt at the Dairy Queen.	He turns and runs away.	He forgets to pay attention to his surroundings.
Charlie is lost and alone.	He is scared to open his eyes.	He cries out so someone might hear him.

Question 3, Part B: D.

Question 4: B.

Question 5: C.

Question 6: C. and E.

Question 7: B.

Grade 7 Sample Items: "Whitewashing the Fence" from *Tom Sawyer*

Question 1: A.

Question 2: B.

Question 3: D.

Question 4, Part A: E.

Question 4, Part B: C.

Question 5, Part A: A. and E.

Question 5, Part B: C.

Question 6:

"Whitewashing is a rewarding experience." There are two possible responses:

13 Tom resumed his whitewashing, and answered carelessly: "Well, maybe it is, and maybe it ain't. All I know, is it suits Tom Sawyer."

16 "Like it? Well, I don't see why I oughtn't to like it. Does a boy get a chance to whitewash a fence every day?" That put the thing in a new light. Ben stopped nibbling his apple. Tom swept his brush daintily back and forth—stepped back to note the effect—added a touch here and there—criticized the effect again—Ben watching every move and getting more and more interested, more and more absorbed. Presently he said:

"Whitewashing requires special skill." There are two possible answers.

19 "No—no—I reckon it wouldn't hardly do, Ben. You see, Aunt Polly's awful particular about this fence—right here on the street, you know—but if it was the back fence I wouldn't mind and SHE wouldn't. Yes, she's awful particular about this fence; it's got to be done very careful; I reckon there ain't one boy in a thousand, maybe two thousand, that can do it the way it's got to be done."

21 "Ben, I'd like to, honest injun; but Aunt Polly—well, Jim wanted to do it, but she wouldn't let him; Sid wanted to do it, and she wouldn't let Sid. Now don't you see how I'm fixed? If you was to tackle this fence and anything was to happen to it—"

Question 7, Part A: B.

Question 7, Part B: C.

Grade 8 Sample Items: from *The Open Boat*

Question 1: B. and E.   Question 4: C. and F.

Question 2: C.   Question 5, Part A: D.

Question 3: A.   Question 5, Part B: C.

Question 6:

"The men have established a deep respect for others in the dinghy" (paragraph 1 or 2); "The men offer encouragement by promoting thoughts of rescue" (paragraph 11 or 12); and "Rations are limited but shared equally" (paragraph 17)

Grade 8 Sample Items: "Dulce et Decorum Est"

Question 1, Part A: D.

Question 1, Part B: A.

Question 2, Part A: B.

Question 2, Part B: A., E., and F.

Question 3, Part A: Lines 15–16 ("In all my dreams before my helpless sight / He plunges at me, guttering. choking, drowning.")

Question 3, Part B: C.

Question 4: C.

Question 5, Part A: Correct answers and textual evidence to support each function:

stanza 1	stanza 2	stanza 4
1. Builds tone by telling horrific details	1. Builds tone by telling horrific details	1. Builds tone by telling horrific details
Evidence: "coughing like hags"; "many had lost their boots, but limped on, blood-shod"	Evidence: "flound'ring like a man in fire or lime"; "He plunges at me, guttering, choking, drowning"	Evidence: "watch the white eyes writhing in his face"; "the blood come gargling from the froth-corrupted lungs"
2. Establishes the war scene	2. Propels the action of the poem	2. States the speaker's view of war
Evidence: "on the haunting flares we turned our backs"; "the hoots of gas-shells dropping softly behind"	Evidence: "Gas! GAS! Quick, boys!"; "I saw him drowning"	Evidence: "you would not tell with such high zest"; "The old Lie: _Dulce et decorum est / Pro patria mori._"
3. Characterizes the soldiers as weary	3. Introduces the speaker of the poem	
Evidence: "bent double"; "men marched asleep"; "drunk with fatigue"	Evidence: "I saw him drowning"; "In all my dreams before my helpless sight/He plunges at me"	

Evidence added to direct students back to the text, if necessary.

Question 5, Part B: A.

Question 6: B.

Question 7: A., C., and G.

References

Adams, Marilyn Jager. "The Challenge of Advanced Texts: The Interdependence of Reading and Learning," in *Reading More, Reading Better: Are American Students Reading Enough of the Right Stuff?*, ed. E. H. Hiebert. New York, NY: Guilford Press, 2009, 163–189.

Adler, Ronald B., Lawrence B. Rosenfeld, and Russell F. *Proctor II. Interplay: The Process of Interpersonal Communicating (8th edition). Fort Worth, TX: Harcourt, 2001.*

Allam, Court. "Five Close Reading Strategies to Support the Common Core," *iTeach. iCoach. iBlog* (blog), June 11, 2012, accessed January 28, 2015,

   http://iteachicoachiblog.blogspot.com/2012/06/five-simple-close-reading-strategies.html

Allen, Janet. *Yellow Brick Roads: Shared and Guided Paths to Independent Reading, 4–12.* Portland, ME: Stenhouse Publishers. 2000, accessed May 11, 2015,

   http://www.readwritethink.org/professional-development/strategy-guides/shared-reading-opportunities-direct-30823.html

Allen Simon, Cathy. "Using the Think-Pair-Share Technique," *ReadWriteThink*, International Reading Association and National Council of Teachers of English, 2015, accessed January 28, 2015,

   http://www.readwritethink.org/professional-development/strategy-guides/using-think-pair-share-30626.html.

American College Testing. *ACT College and Career Readiness Standards—Writing.* Iowa City, IA: American College Testing, 2014, accessed May 11, 2015,

   http://www.act.org/standard/planact/pdf/WritingStandards.pdf.

American College Testing. *Reading Between the Lines: What the ACT Reveals about College Readiness in Reading.* Iowa City, IA: American College Testing, 2006, accessed January 28, 2015,

   http://www.act.org/research/policymakers/pdf/reading_report.pdf.

Anderson, Richard C., Elfrieda H. Hiebert, Judith A. Scott, and Ian A. G. Wilkinson. *Becoming a Nation of Readers: The Report of the Commission on Reading.* Champaign-Urbana, IL: U. S. Department of Education: Center for the Study of Reading, 1985, accessed February 15, 2015,

   http://files.eric.ed.gov/fulltext/ED253865.pdf.

Beck, Isabel L., Margaret G. McKeown, and Linda Kucan. *Bringing Words to Life: Robust Vocabulary Instruction.* New York, NY: Guilford Press, 2002.

Beck, I. L., M.G. McKeown, and L. Kucan. *Creating Robust Vocabulary: Frequently Asked Questions and Extended Examples.* New York, NY: Guilford, 2008.

Blatner, Adam. "Role Playing in Education," last modified October 18, 2009, accessed January 28, 2015,

   http://www.blatner.com/adam/pdntbk/rlplayedu.htm.

Boutelier, Stefani. "What Is Expository Text? Definition, Types & Examples,"*Study.com,* accessed January 28, 2015,

   http://study.com/academy/lesson/what-is-expository-text-definition-types-examples.html#lesson.

Boyles, Nancy. "Closing in on Close Reading." *Educational Leadership* 70, no. 4 (2012): 36–41, accessed January 28, 2015,

    http://www.ascd.org/publications/educational-leadership/dec12/vol70/num04/Closing-in-on-Close-Reading.aspx.

Brown, Sheila and Lee Kappes. *Implementing the Common Core State Standards: A Primer on "Close Reading of Text,"* Washington, DC: The Aspen Institute, 2012, accessed January 28, 2015,

    http://www.aspendrl.org/portal/browse/DocumentDetail?documentId=1396&download.

Burack, Jonathan. "Interpreting Political Cartoons in the History Classroom," *Teaching History*, 2010, accessed January 28, 2015,

    http://teachinghistory.org/teaching-materials/teaching-guides/21733.

Button, Kathryn and Margaret Johnson. "The Role of Shared Reading in Developing Effective Early Reading Strategies." *Reading Horizons* 37, no. 4 (1997): 262–273.

Carlisle, Joanne F. *Fostering Vocabulary: Development in Elementary Classrooms.* Ann Arbor, MI: University of Michigan/Center for the Improvement of Early Reading Achievement (CIERA), 2002.

College Board. *Test Specifications for the Redesigned SAT.* Princeton, NJ: College Board, 2014, accessed January 28, 2015,

    https://www.collegeboard.org/sites/default/files/test_specifications_for_the_redesigned_sat_na3.pdf.

College Entrance Examination Board. *Writing: A Ticket to Work...or a Ticket Out. Report of the National Commission on Writing (for America's Families, Schools, and Colleges.)* Princeton, NJ: College Entrance Examination Board, 2004, accessed March 4, 2015,

    http://www.collegeboard.com/prod_downloads/writingcom/writing-ticket-to-work.pdf.

Dale, E. & O'Rourke, J. *Vocabulary Building.* Columbus, OH: Zaner-Bloser, 1986.

"Displaying Data," *TeacherVision*, accessed March 9, 2015,

    https://www.teachervision.com/skill-builder/graphs-and-charts/48945.html.

Fisher, Douglas. "Close Reading and the CCSS—Part 1: Video Clip and Transcript," *Common Core State Standards Toolbox for English Language Arts and Literacy. McGraw Hill Education*, last modified 2012, accessed February 15, 2015,

    http://www.mhecommoncoretoolbox.com/close-reading-and-the-ccss-part-1.html.

Fisher, Douglas, and Nancy Frey. "Close Reading in Elementary Schools." *The Reading Teacher,* 66, no. 3 (2012): 179–188. Doi:10.1002/TRTR.01117, accessed January 28, 2015,

    http://fisherandfrey.com/uploads/posts/Close_Reading_Elem.pdf.

Fisher, Douglas, Nancy Frey, and Diane Lapp. *Text Complexity: Raising Rigor in Reading.* Newark, DE: International Reading Association, 2012.

Florida Department of Education, "Closing the Summer Reading Gap for Secondary Students: Parent Resources," last modified 2011, accessed March 9, 2015,

    http://mclane.mysdhc.org/mclane%20information/SummerReading-parent%20resources.pdf.

Fountas, Irene C. and Gay Sue Pinnell. *Guided Reading: Good First Teaching for All Children.* Portsmouth, NH: Heinemann, 1996.

Giovanoni, Susan, Michi Hanaoka, and Natalie Pascarella. Performing Arts and Literacy: A Study in the Effects of Music, Dance, and Acting on Early-Childhood Literacy, last modified 2010, accessed January 28, 2015,

https://files.nyu.edu/sg2747/public/perform.html.

Global Language Monitor. *Number of Words in the English Language: 1,025,109.8.* Global Language Monitor, last modified 2014, accessed January 28, 2015,

http://www.languagemonitor.com/number-of-words/
number-of-words-in-the-english-language-1008879/.

The Glossary of Education Reform. Critical Friend: Definition, 2013, accessed on March 9, 2015,

http://edglossary.org/critical-friend/.

Graham, S. and M. A. Hebert. *Writing to Read: Evidence for How Writing Can Improve Reading. A Carnegie Corporation Time to Act Report.* Washington, DC: Alliance for Excellent Education, 2010, accessed January 28, 2015,

http://carnegie.org/fileadmin/Media/Publications/WritingToRead_01.pdf.

Graham, S., A. Bollinger, C. Booth Olson, C. D'Aoust, C. MacArthur, D. McCutchen, and N. Olinghouse. *Teaching Elementary School Students to Be Effective Writers: A Practice Guide* (NCEE 2012-4058). Washington, DC: National Center for Education Evaluation and Regional Assistance, Institute of Education Sciences, U.S. Department of Education, 2012, accessed January 28, 2015,

http://ies.ed.gov/ncee/wwc/pdf/practice_guides/writing_pg_062612.pdf.

Graham, Steve and Dolores Perin. *Writing Next: Effective Strategies to Improve Writing of Adolescents in Middle and High Schools—A Report to Carnegie Corporation of New York.* Washington, DC: Alliance for Excellent Education, 2007.

Heberle, Manuela. "What Is Active Listening? Techniques, Definition & Examples— Supplemental Lesson," *Study.com*, accessed March 15, 2015,

http://study.com/academy/lesson/what-is-active-listening-techniques-definition-examples.html.

Hiebert, Elfrieda H. *Seven Actions That Teachers Can Take Right Now: Text Complexity.* Santa Cruz, CA: Text Project and the University of California, 2012, accessed January 28, 2015,

http://textproject.org/professional-development/
text-matters/7-actions-that-teachers-can-take-right-now-text-complexity.

Hirsch, Jr., E.D. "Reading Comprehension Requires Knowledge—of Words and the World: Scientific Insights into the Fourth-Grade Slump and the Nation's Stagnant Comprehension Scores." *American Educator,* Spring 2003, 10–22, 28–29, 44–45. Washington, DC: American Federation of Teachers, accessed March 9, 2015,

http://www.aft.org/sites/default/files/periodicals/Hirsch.pdf.

Juel, Connie and Rebecca Deffes. "Making Words Stick." *The Best of Educational Leadership 2003–2004,* 61(6), 30–34. Alexandria, VA: Association for Supervision and Curriculum Development, accessed January 28, 2015,

http://www.ascd.org/publications/educational-leadership/summer04/vol61/num09/
Making-Words-Stick.aspx.

Liben, David. *Aspects of Text Complexity: Vocabulary Research Base*. Chicago, IL: Bill & Melinda Gates Foundation, 2010, accessed March 31, 2015,
http://docs.gatesfoundation.org/edextranet/documents/
literacyconveningvocabularyresearchbase.pdf_br.

Liben, David. *Why Complex Text Matters: Aspects of Text Complexity Project*. Washington, DC: Council of Chief State School Officers, 2010, accessed January 28, 2015,
http://www.ccsso.org/Documents/Text%20Complexity/Check%20the%20Specs/
Why%20Complex%20Text%20Matters.pdf.

Liben, Meredith and David Liben. *Complete Guide to Creating Text-Dependent Questions*. New York: Student Achievement Partners, 2013, accessed January 28, 2015,
http://achievethecore.org/page/46/
complete-guide-to-creating-text-dependent-questions-detail-pg.

MassBay Community College Academic Achievement Center. *Strategies for Answering Reading Questions*, 2005, accessed on March 31, 2015,
http://www.massbay.edu/uploadedFiles/Admissions_and_Financial_Aid/Enrollment/
QUESTIONTYPE.pdf

McClennen, S.A. "Dr. McClennen's Close Reading Guide: How to Do a Close Reading," 2001 (site updated 2003), accessed January 28, 2015,
http://personal.psu.edu/users/s/a/sam50/closeread.htm.

Merriam-Webster Dictionary, accessed January 28, 2015,
http://www.merriam-webster.com/dictionary/writing.

Nagy, W. and R. C. Anderson. "How Many Words Are There in Printed School English?" *Reading Research Quarterly*, 19 (1984): 304–330.
http://reading.uoregon.edu/big_ideas/voc/voc_what.php#research

National Center for Education Statistics. *The Condition of Education 2014* (NCES 2014-083). Washington, DC: U.S. Department of Education, National Center for Education Statistics, 2014, accessed January 28, 2015,
http://nces.ed.gov/programs/coe/indicator_cpa.asp.

National Centre of Literacy and Numeracy for Adults. "Academic Vocabulary." Hamilton, New Zealand: National Centre of Literacy and Numeracy for Adults, 2012, accessed January 28, 2015,
http://www.literacyandnumeracyforadults.com/resources/354996.

National Commission on Writing in America's Schools and Colleges. *The Neglected "R": The Need for a Writing Revolution. Report of the National Commission on Writing in America's Schools and Colleges*. Princeton, NJ: College Entrance Examination Board, 2003, accessed January 28, 2015,
http://www.collegeboard.com/prod_downloads/writingcom/neglectedr.pdf.

National Governors Association Center for Best Practices and Council of Chief State School Officers. *Common Core State Standards for English Language Arts and Literacy in History/Social Studies, Science, and Technical Subjects*. Washington, DC: Authors, 2010, accessed December 6, 2014,
http://www.corestandards.org/ELA-Literacy/.

National Governors Association Center for Best Practices and Council of Chief State School Officers. *Common Core State Standards for English Language Arts and Literacy in History/Social Studies, Science, and Technical Subjects—Appendix A: Research Supporting Key Elements of the Standards*. Washington, DC: Authors, 2010, accessed December 6, 2014,
http://www.corestandards.org/assets/Appendix_A.pdf.

National Institute of Child Health and Human Development. *Report of the National Reading Panel: Teaching Children to Read: An Evidence-Based Assessment of the Scientific Research Literature on Reading and Its Implications for Reading Instruction* (NIH Publication No. 00–4769). Washington, DC: U.S. Government Printing Office, 2000, accessed January 28, 2015,
http://www.nichd.nih.gov/publications/pubs/nrp/Documents/report.pdf.

National Reading Technical Assistance Center. *A Review of the Current Research on Vocabulary Instruction: A Research Synthesis*. Washington, DC: RMC Research Corporation, 2010, accessed January 28, 2015,
http://www2.ed.gov/programs/readingfirst/support/rmcfinal1.pdf.

Neuman, Susan B., Carol Copple, and Sue Bredekamp. *Learning to Read and Write: Developmentally Appropriate Practices for Young Children*. Washington, DC: National Association for the Education of Young Children, 2000, accessed January 28, 2015,
http://www.readingrockets.org/article/reading-aloud-build-comprehension.

Partnership for the Assessment of Readiness for College and Careers (PARCC). *Passage Selection Guidelines for Assessing CCSS ELA*, 2012, accessed March 31, 2015,
http://parcconline.org/ela-literacy-test-documents.

Partnership for 21st Century Skills. *Framework for 21st Century Learning*, 2011, accessed January 28, 2015,
http://www.p21.org/about-us/p21-framework/264.

Pressley, Michael. "Comprehension Instruction: What Makes Sense Now, What Might Make Sense Soon." *Reading Online*, last modified 2000, accessed February 15, 2015,
http://readingonline.org/articles/handbook/pressley/index.html.

Routman, Regie. *Conversations: Strategies for Teaching, Learning, and Evaluating*. Portsmouth, NH: Heinemann, 2000, accessed January 28, 2015,
http://www.heinemann.com/shared/onlineresources/e00109/chapter2.pdf.

Sedita, Joan. "Effective Vocabulary Instruction." *Insights on Learning Disabilities*, 2(1), 33–45. Rowley, MA: Keys to Literacy, 2005.
http://www.keystoliteracy.com/wp-content/uploads/2012/08/effective-vocabulary-instruction.pdf

Shanahan, Timothy. "You Want Me to Read What?" *Educational Leadership* 71(3) (2013): 10–15, accessed March 8, 2015,
http://www.educationalleadership-digital.com/educationalleadership/201311#pg18.

"Shared Reading," *Reading Rockets*, accessed March 9, 2015,
http://www.readingrockets.org/strategies/shared_reading.

Stahl, Steven A. "How Words Are Learned Incrementally Over Multiple Exposures." *American Educator*. Spring 2003. 27(1): 18–19, 44–45.

"Strategies for Inferencing," *Reading Rockets*, accessed January 28, 2015,
   http://www.readingrockets.org/strategies/inference.

Student Achievement Partners. "Checklist for Evaluating Question Quality." New York: Achieve the Core, 2013, accessed January 28, 2015,
   http://achievethecore.org/page/47/checklist-for-evaluating-question-quality-detail-pg.

Student Achievement Partners. "Introduction to the ELA/Literacy Shifts of the Common Core State Standards (PowerPoint)." New York: Achieve the Core, 2015, accessed May 11, 2015,
   http://docs.google.com/viewerng/viewer?url=http://achievethecore.org/content/
   upload/2.intro_to_ela_literacy_shifts_presentation_slides_with_notes_ATC_
   updated_11_7_13.ppt

Sweeney, S. M. & Mason, P. A. *Research-based Practices in Vocabulary Instruction: An Analysis of What Works in Grades PreK–12*. Boston, MA: Studies & Research Committee of the Massachusetts Reading Association, August 2011, accessed January 28, 2015,
   http://massreading.org/wp-content/uploads/2013/08/vocpaper.pdf.

Texas Reading Initiative. *Promoting Vocabulary Development: Components of Effective Vocabulary Instruction* (Revised edition). Austin, TX: Texas Education Agency, 2002, accessed January 28, 2015,
   http://resources.buildingrti.utexas.org/PDF/redbk5.pdf.

The Vermont Writing Collaborative, with Student Achievement Partners and Council of Chief State School Officers. *In Common: Effective Writing for All Students Collection of All Student Work Samples—K–12*. New York: Achieve the Core, 2013, accessed January 28, 2015,
   http://achievethecore.org/file/all/507.

Varlas, Laura. "Academic Vocabulary Builds Student Achievement." *ASCD Education Update*, November 2012: 1–4, 5, accessed January 28, 2015,
   http://www.ascd.org/publications/newsletters/education-update/nov12/vol54/num11/
   Academic-Vocabulary-Builds-Student-Achievement.aspx.

"Vocabulary Research Says: Vocabulary Gap," *University of Oregon Center on Teaching and Learning*. Accessed from website March 1, 2015,
   http://reading.uoregon.edu/big_ideas/voc/voc_what.php#research.

White, Jan V. *Using Charts and Graphs: 1,000 Ideas for Visual Persuasion*. New York and London: R.R. Bowker Company, 1984, accessed March 1, 2015,
   http://ia802703.us.archive.org/11/items/usingchartsgraph00whit/
   usingchartsgraph00whit.pdf.

Wilkinson, Louise C. and Elaine R. Silliman. "Classroom Language and Literacy Learning," *Reading Online*, last modified 2000, accessed February 15, 2015,
   http://readingonline.org/articles/handbook/wilkinson/.

Wilson, Leslie Owen. "Five Basic Types of Questions," *The Second Principle*, 2015, accessed January 28, 2015,
   http://thesecondprinciple.com/teaching-essentials/five-basic-types-questions/.

Wisconsin Department of Public Instruction, *Wisconsin Common Core State Standards for English Language Arts*, 2012, accessed March 9, 2015,
   http://standards.dpi.wi.gov/sites/default/files/imce/cal/pdf/vocabulary.pdf.

References for Summative ELA Assessment Items

Grade 3:

"The Fisherman and His Wife" Set. Public Domain

Student Achievement Partners. *Grade 3 Mini-Assessment Set—"The Fisherman and His Wife" by Jacob and Wilhelm Grimm, translated by Lucy Crane.* Accessed March 20, 2015, from Achieve the Core ELA/Literacy Grades 3–5 Annotated Mini-Assessments, pages 3–16.
   http://achievethecore.org/content/upload/Fisherman_and_his_Wife_Set_3MA.pdf

Lexile—Scene 1: 1320; Lexile—Scene 2: 1390; Lexile—Scene 3: 1380; Lexile—Scene 4: 1390

Grade 4:

The Velveteen Rabbit Or How Toys Become Real. Public Domain by Margery Williams

Williams, Margery. *The Velveteen Rabbit.* Garden City, NY: Doubleday and Company, 1922. Public Domain. Accessed on March 20, 2015, from Project Gutenberg.
   http://www.gutenberg.org/cache/epub/11757/pg11757.txt

Grade 5:

The Summer of the Swans Pair

Student Achievement Partners. *Mini-Assessment for Two Excerpts from "The Summer of the Swans" by Betsy Byars.* Accessed March 9, 2015, from Achieve the Core ELA/Literacy Grades 3–5 Annotated Mini-Assessments, pages 3–7.
   http://achievethecore.org/page/830/
   mini-assessment-for-two-excerpts-from-the-summer-of-the-swans-by-betsy-byars-
   detail-pg

Lexile—Excerpt 1: 1110; Lexile—Excerpt 2: 950

Grade 6:

Jaques' Soliloquy from *As You Like It* (Act II, Scene vii) by William Shakespeare. Public Domain

Student Achievement Partners. *Close Reading Model Lesson for "As You Like It" by William Shakespeare.* Accessed February 15, 2015, from Achieve the Core ELA/Literacy Close Reading Model Lessons, Grades 6–8, pages 3, 12.
   http://achievethecore.org/page/21/as-you-like-it-by-william-shakespeare-detail-pg

Lexile: 1280 (text is relevant for grades 6–8)

Grade 7:

"Whitewashing the Fence" from *Tom Sawyer* by Mark Twain. Public Domain

Student Achievement Partners. *Close Reading Model Lesson for "The Glorious Whitewasher" from The Adventures of Tom Sawyer by Mark Twain (with Mini-Assessment).* Accessed February 15, 2015, from Achieve the Core ELA/Literacy Grades 6–8 Annotated Mini-Assessments, pages 12, 14–19.

> http://achievethecore.org/page/22/
> the-glorious-whitewasher-from-the-adventures-of-tom-sawyer-by-mark-twain-with-mini-
> assessment-detail-pg

Lexile—810 (Despite this grade 4/5 level, the language and conventions, as well as the sophisticated use of plot, push this text well into grade 7, as some of the words may be inaccessible for students unused to dealing with archaic language and complex sentences. The theme is obvious and well developed throughout the text.)

Narrative of the Life of Frederick Douglass, an American Slave, Written by Himself (1845) by Frederick Douglass. Public Domain

Student Achievement Partners. *Close Reading Model Lesson for "Narrative of the Life of Frederick Douglass" by Frederick Douglass.* Accessed February 15, 2015, from Achieve the Core ELA/Literacy Close Reading Model Lessons, Grade 8 (relevant for grades 7–9), pages 3–4, 11.

> http://achievethecore.org/page/32/
> narrative-of-the-life-of-frederick-douglass-by-frederick-douglass-detail-pg

Grade 8:

Chapter III from *The Open Boat* by Stephen Crane. Public Domain

Student Achievement Partners. *Mini-Assessment for Chapter III from "The Open Boat" by Stephen Crane.* Accessed February 15, 2015, from Achieve the Core ELA/Literacy Grades 6–8 Annotated Mini-Assessments, pages 3–8.

> http://achievethecore.org/page/829/
> mini-assessment-for-chapter-iii-from-the-open-boat-by-stephen-crane-detail-pg

Lexile: 1180

"Dulce et Decorum Est" by Wilfred Owen and "Who's for the Game?" by Jessie Pope. Public Domain

Student Achievement Partners. *Mini-Assessment for "Dulce et Decorum Est" by Wilfred Owen and "Who's for the Game" by Jessie Pope.* Accessed February 15, 2015 from Achieve the Core ELA/Literacy Grades 6–8 Annotated Mini-Assessments, pages 3–9.

> http://achievethecore.org/page/23/
> dulce-et-decorum-est-by-wilfred-owen-with-mini-assessment-detail-pg

"Dulce et Decorum Est" Lexile: 1200

Maupin House *by*
capstone
professional

At Maupin House by Capstone Professional, we continue to look for professional development resources that support grades K–8 classroom teachers in areas, such as these:

Literacy	**Language Arts**
Content-Area Literacy	**Research-Based Practices**
Assessment	**Inquiry**
Technology	**Differentiation**
Standards-Based Instruction	**School Safety**
Classroom Management	**School Community**

If you have an idea for a professional development resource, visit our Become an Author website at:

   http://maupinhouse.com/index.php/become-an-author

There are two ways to submit questions and proposals.

1. You may send them electronically to:

   http://maupinhouse.com/index.php/become-an-author

2. You may send them via postal mail. Please be sure to include a self-addressed stamped envelope for us to return materials.

   Acquisitions Editor
   Capstone Professional
   1 N. LaSalle Street, Suite 1800
   Chicago, IL 60602